Colonial Taverns

OF

NEW JERSEY

Colonial Taverns

OF

NEW JERSEY

LIBATIONS, LIBERTY & REVOLUTION

MICHAEL C. GABRIELE

THE
History
PRESS

Published by The History Press
Charleston, SC
www.historypress.com

Opposite: *Tavern Scene*, painting by Johann-Baptist Pflug, 1827. *Public domain.*

First published 2023

Manufactured in the United States

ISBN 9781467148962

Library of Congress Control Number: 2022949652

There is no private house in which people can enjoy themselves so well as at a capital tavern. The master of the house is anxious to entertain his guests; the guests are anxious to be agreeable to him, and no man, but a very impudent dog indeed, can as freely command what is in another man's house, as if it were his own. Whereas at a tavern, there is a general freedom from anxiety. You are sure you are welcome, and the more noise you make, the more trouble you give, the more good things you call for, the welcomer you are. No servants (from a private residence) will attend you with the alacrity [cheerful readiness], which [tavern] waiters do, who are incited by the prospect of an immediate reward, in proportion as they please. No sir, there is nothing which has yet been contrived by man, by which so much happiness is produced, as by a good tavern or inn.[1]

—Samuel Johnson (1709–1784),
eighteenth-century British literary figure

CONTENTS

ACKNOWLEDGEMENTS

Special thanks and appreciation goes to Jennifer Dowling Norato for her peer review of this book. Norato is a former chapter regent and current member of the Daughters of the American Revolution (DAR), who has proudly documented several of her Patriot ancestors. She is the New Jersey chapter president of the Alexander Hamilton Awareness Society, a published author, a teacher with the Emerson public school district and a graduate of Ramapo College, and she earned a master's degree in history and social sciences from Montclair State University.

Jennifer Dowling Norato. *Photo courtesy of J. Norato.*

Thank you to all of the individuals and organizations that generously provided information and images for this publication. They're listed in the back of this book. Thank you to my publisher, Arcadia Publishing/The History Press, especially my colleagues Katie Parry, J. Banks Smither and Zoe Ames, for giving me the opportunity to write another book on New Jersey history. I'm most grateful for their support and guidance. Thank you to my wife, Julia, for her assistance during Garden State road trips.

Your most humble and obedient servant,
M. Gabriele

Note: All towns, landmarks and events mentioned in this book are located in New Jersey unless otherwise indicated.

A STATE, NOT A COLONY

Inside a Haddonfield tavern, 246 years ago, the colony of New Jersey declared itself to be a state.

In 1777, the Revolutionary War was well underway, and these were dangerous days in New Jersey. At the time, William Livingston, a staunch Patriot and brigadier general in New Jersey's militia, served as governor of the state. Members of the General Assembly of the State of New Jersey met at the House of Hugh Creighton tavern in Haddonfield on Saturday, September 20, 1777, in a room on the second floor. They enacted legislation "to establish the word *State* instead of *Colony* in commissions, writs and other process."[2]

And whereas since the framing of the said Constitution, the honorable congress has declared the United Colonies free and independent States; And also whereas since the Declaration of Independency, the commissions and writs have run in the name of the State, and not of the Colony of New-Jersey, and indictments have concluded against the peace of this state and not of this colony, and some doubts may arise respecting the validity of the commissions, writs and indictments to as aforesaid worded; BE IT THEREFORE ENACTED by the authority aforesaid that, from and after the publication of this act, all commissions and writs which by the Constitution are required to run in the name of the Colony shall run in the name of the State of New-Jersey; and all indictments shall conclude against the peace of this State, the government and dignity of the same; and that all commissions writs and indictments heretofore issued, preferred and

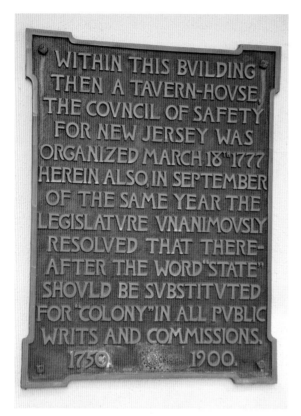

Left: Plaque on Indian King Tavern, Haddonfield. *Photo by M. Gabriele.*

Below: Second-floor meeting room, Indian King Tavern, Haddonfield. *Photo by M. Gabriele.*

Opposite: Indian King Tavern, Haddonfield. *Photo by M. Gabriele.*

exhibited, which have the word State and not the word Colony, shall be, and
they hereby are declared to be good and effectual in the law.
Passed at Haddonfield, September 20, 1777.

The September 20 statement went a step beyond legislation from a year earlier. New Jersey's provincial congress had met at the Blue Anchor Tavern in Burlington on July 2, 1776, "agreed upon a set of charter rights" and adopted an elected representative form of government—its first state constitution—in effect declaring independence from Britain.[3]

Whereas George the Third, king of Great Britain, has refused protection
to the good people of these colonies; and, by assenting to sundry acts of the
British parliament, attempted to subject them to the absolute dominion of that
body; and has also made war upon them, in the most cruel and unnatural
manner, for no other cause, than asserting their just rights, all civil authority
under him is necessarily at an end, and a dissolution of government in each
colony has consequently taken place. And whereas, in the present deplorable
situation of these colonies, exposed to the fury of a cruel and relentless enemy,
some form of government is absolutely necessary, not only for the preservation
of good order, but also the more effectually to unite the people, and enable them
to exert their whole force in their own necessary defense.

Linda Hess and Michelle Hughes, the historic interpreters at Haddonfield's Indian King Tavern (the current name of the building previously known as the House of Hugh Creighton), said in an August 2021 interview that the General Assembly members must have realized the gravity of the situation. The British king, King George III, would have understood that the September 20, 1777 statement was a treasonous move. Today, in retrospect, the legislation stands out as a bold proclamation on independence and New Jersey's patriotic aspirations. However, Hughes and Hess point out that there is interpretation to consider, given the context of events in 1777. The declaration of "state, not colony" was one item among several on the legislative docket that day. Members of the general assembly were aware of the political tensions that existed in New Jersey. Many Loyalists, also known as Tories, resided in the state and wanted to remain united with the British Crown. The two Indian King historic interpreters described the statement of September 20, 1777, as one significant piece of a complex puzzle for New Jersey's role in the American Revolution.

"SOCIAL AND POLITICAL CENTERS OF UNRIVALED IMPORTANCE"

New Jersey was the "Crossroads of the American Revolution." Taverns housed the daily experiences of people during the colonial era, and their stories provide a window into the state's history from that period. The aim of this book is to unearth those long-forgotten tales. The meeting in Haddonfield is just one example of the importance of taverns during New Jersey's colonial days. In many cases, taverns were the only places where momentous events and gatherings could occur. Taverns were havens for Patriots as well as Loyalists. Because taverns were public venues, political operatives on both sides of the Patriot/Loyalist divide could meet, discuss plans and, in effect, hide in plain sight. The original Green Dragon Tavern in Boston was a favorite gathering place for the Sons of Liberty and other Massachusetts Patriots.[4]

Richard P. McCormick, PhD, the late professor emeritus of history at Rutgers University, writes that New Jersey's colonial taverns were "social and political centers of unrivaled importance. Public meetings, balls, elections and celebrations were held there, and the taproom was constantly enlivened by the presence of local gentry, assembled for gossip and frivolity. Probably

Village Tavern, painting by John Lewis Krimmel, 1813–14. *Courtesy of the Toledo Museum of Art.*

no other institution played such a lively and vital role [as the tavern] in colonial society."[5]

Author Leonard Lundin, PhD, observes that "[General] George Washington's daring and military skill and the corresponding blunders of the British commanders were of first importance, but the attitude of Jerseymen themselves helped to weight the scales." Taverns were frequently used by Washington as a headquarters, and tavern keepers aided Continental army soldiers. Along with food, soldiers craved alcohol to ease their misery during the war. One Continental army general, in a letter to Washington expressing the discontent among soldiers stationed in Princeton in February 1777, wrote that "we were some days without rum, when a fresh supply came they expected to receive all their back rations at once. This, however, I would not comply with, for…there would be not a man of them fit for duty." Lundin indicated that some members of the company "went off to slake their thirst in more congenial surroundings," which most likely meant finding a Princeton tavern.[6]

Taverns became recruitment stations for colonial militias and provided a meeting place for local committees of safety. Historian Kieran O'Keefe, PhD, states that "while the most famous scenes of the American Revolutionary

Reenactors portraying Bergen County militia members, led by Colonel Theunis Dey (*far right*), at Dey Mansion Washington's Headquarters, Wayne. *Photo by M. Gabriele.*

War involve major battles or deliberations in Congress, the driving forces behind the Revolution within small towns were committees of safety. As the war progressed and British authority dissipated, these committees became the effective government in most localities until the formal establishment of state governments. They had responsibilities such as regulating the economy, suppressing Loyalists, procuring military supplies, raising revolutionary forces, and overseeing civil and criminal justice."[7]

Mark Edward Lender, PhD, professor emeritus of history at Kean University and a prolific author, writes that "by the end of the war for independence, New Jersey tax records noted the existence of 443 taverns spread fairly evenly across the state." Colonial taverns in New Jersey, Lender points out, were a social and economic necessity. "A trip from New York to Philadelphia took several days by stagecoach, and those on the road needed places to stay as well as food and drink. Coach and wagon drivers, passengers, and individual travelers depended on the network of taverns that lined the main transportation routes across the province. Similarly, most ferry docks were only steps from an inn." He also identifies the interaction between colonial soldiers and taverns. "New Jersey was the seat of the war between 1776 and 1783, and during these years the state's taverns served thousands of soldiers. The correspondence and journals of Revolutionary soldiers are replete with references to regional taverns."[8]

A TOAST TO THE ASSEMBLY CLAUSE

Baylen J. Linnekin, an author, attorney and senior fellow with the Reason Foundation (Los Angeles and Washington, D.C.), in an article published in the spring 2012 edition of the *Hastings Constitutional Law Quarterly*, traces the de facto origins of the U.S. Constitution's First Amendment "Freedom of Assembly Clause" to the daily gatherings—social, political, conspiratorial, for simple carousing or otherwise—inside of colonial taverns in the lead-up to the Revolutionary War. The common interactions inside of taverns during the 1700s had profound, unintended consequences to establish a fundamental liberty in the United States.[9]

Interviewed in August 2020, Linnekin said his research reveals that "the colonial tavern was the place that inspired the Assembly Clause. Taverns and the town square were the places where people assembled. Taverns were places where travelers would bring news from other places. Sailor stories were told at taverns in port towns." Typically, there were disagreements and debates inside of taverns—two- and three-way conversations, with a variety of points of view. "People were largely entitled to free speech, but you could get in trouble if there were British troops inside of a tavern."

Reenactors pose as colonial citizens, East Jersey Old Town. *Photo by M. Gabriele.*

Linnekin described the role played by colonial citizens assembling in taverns in fostering the freedom of assembly and in combating growing British attacks on the rights of American colonists.

The First Amendment to the Constitution is a cluster of distinct but related rights. The freedom of assembly protected therein is one right that Americans exercise every day. With perhaps the exception of speech, assembly is the most widely and commonly practiced action that is enumerated in the Bill of Rights. The proper situs [a place where something originates] *of the Assembly Clause, research reveals, is in its birthplace: colonial America's taverns. Colonial taverns served not just as establishments for drinking alcohol, but as vital centers where colonists of reputations great and small gathered to read printed tracts, speak with one another on important issues of the day, debate the news, organize boycotts, draft treatises and demands, plot the expulsion of their British overlords, and establish a new nation.*

In his article for the *Hastings Constitutional Law Quarterly*, Linnekin writes that, apart from the drink and food they provided, taverns served three key roles in colonial life:

> *First, all manner of speech, centered on everything from politics and trade to gossip and scandal, took place in taverns. Scholars have invariably labeled this mishmash of vital discourse between and among colonists [as] informal talk or "tavern talk." The second key role played by taverns was as the primary news source in the colonies. In fact, taverns were the most important place colonists could assemble to hear and debate the news and to learn about the outside world. The third vital role that colonial taverns played was as hubs of colonial assembly. Taverns were the only colonial space outside the home that permitted participants in all social classes the opportunity to decide whether, how and to what extent they would participate and shape their interactions with others. Taverns fostered a deep sense of community and offered the perfect milieu for political debate. In this way, taverns served as political spaces where citizens could participate in civic life.*

The spirited social interaction at taverns provided a thin veil of cover for patrons attempting to keep a low profile to discreetly craft their political plans. "Groups that comprised colonial civil society, including some agitating for independence, often held their regular meetings in taverns so as to avoid the appearance that their groups were some sort of secret society," Linnekin writes. "The news, speech and assembly that the tavern *situs* could provide and facilitate were key in fostering the burgeoning colonial movement toward independence. Taverns [were the places] where British tyranny was condemned, militiamen organized and independence plotted."

Linnekin goes on to write,

> *[The] speech and action that dominated colonial taverns were shaped by an awareness of the tavern as public space. The concept of place is a fundamental aspect of the freedom of assembly. And the tavern was the place in colonial America that equalized assembly rights more than any other. Colonial taverns served the classic First Amendment role of breeding an alert, active citizenry. They not only shaped discourse, but were central to the formation of public opinion. As a result, booze-filled gatherings in taverns were where shared American values were forged and affirmed.*

Statue of George Washington, Morristown Green. *Photo by M. Gabriele.*

If there are any doubts regarding the importance of colonial taverns, consider George Washington's September 14, 1787 entry in his journal.[10]

Friday 14th
Attended Convention.
Dined at the City Tavern.

Philadelphia hosted the Constitutional Convention, which ran from May 14 to September 17, 1787. Delegates assembled to finalize details on the American "experiment" of a constitutional democratic republic. The gathering was "the hundred-day debate [that] would set the United States on the course towards becoming a true Constitutional Republic." The attendees picked Washington to preside at this grand forum, and they adopted the Constitution on September 17, 1787. Three days earlier, on Friday night, September 14, 1787, delegates held a gala reception to honor Washington at Philadelphia's City Tavern, located at the corner of South Second Avenue and Walnut Street, which had opened in late 1773.[11]

The celebratory spirit of the evening would have included numerous toasts, proclamations and long-winded speeches. Various sources estimate that fifty-five attendees at the City Tavern consumed fifty-four bottles of Madeira wine, sixty bottles of claret wine, eight bottles of whiskey, twenty-two bottles of porter, eight bottles of hard cider, twelve bottles of beer and seven bowls of alcoholic punch. In 2018, Business Insider estimated that the one-night tab (in 2018 dollars) would have totaled more than $17,000.[12]

Hopefully, one of the Founding Fathers left an appropriate tip.

CHAPTER 1

"BETWIXT PERTHTOWN AND BURLINGTON"

"Send Someone to Set Up a Brew House"

When they first set foot in the New World in the 1600s, the colonial proprietors quickly recognized the business potential of New Jersey's verdant landscape and natural resources. They also appreciated the gentlemanly pleasures of alcohol consumption. Gawen Lawric, a London merchant, arrived in East New Jersey in late 1683 to serve as deputy governor under Robert Barclay, a Scottish Quaker theologian, who was the proprietary governor of East Jersey. Not long after settling in at Elizabethtown (present-day Elizabeth), Lawrie wasted little time in writing to his British chums about life in the colony. Two of Lawrie's letters to his colleagues in London, written in January 1684, describe the bounty of New Jersey and encourage his friends to join him in this new realm.[13]

In his first letter, dated January 1, Lawrie writes of drinking cider, "plentiful and good," for one penny per quart. "Good drink that is made of water and molasses, stands in about two shillings per barrel; wholesome, like our eight-shilling beer in England. Eggs [are] three pence per dozen. Vines, walnuts, peaches, strawberries and many other things [are] in the woods." In a second letter, dated January 26, he described eating an abundance of oysters, fish, fowl, pork, beef, venison, Indian corn and oats—but something was missing. "At Amboy, we have one [merchant] setting up to make malt, but we want a brewer. I wish thou would send over someone to set up a brew house and a bake house to bake bread and biscuit."

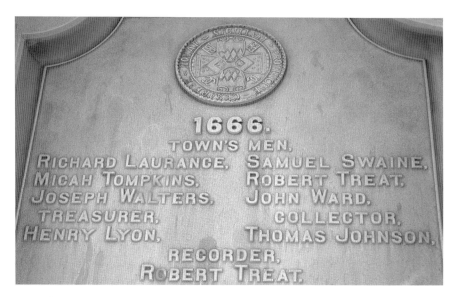

Memorial with the names of Henry Lyon and other Newark founders, Fairmount Cemetery, Newark. *Photo by M. Gabriele.*

Newark held a town meeting in January 1668 and declared that Henry Lyon—who served as the village treasurer from 1668 to 1673—had been chosen to "keep an ordinary for the entertainment of travelers and strangers, and desired him to prepare for it as soon as he can."[14] Based on this date, Lyon is recognized as one of the first operators of a colonial New Jersey tavern. Two years after Lyon opened his hostelry, Thomas Johnson, the Newark constable, also opened a tavern.[15]

"Henry Lyon opened a public house and the constable was appointed to make sure that strong drinks were sold wisely….At that time [Lyon] held the only license to supply alcohol in Newark."[16] Newark needed Lyon to establish a tavern out of necessity. Newark, founded in 1666, was a victim of its own prosperity and popularity as a waterfront colonial village. "The hostel was built to stop visitors from pestering the townsfolk for food, and provide shelter for strangers to the town and regular visitors who might be there on business. It is to be presumed that the planters [farmers] were temperate people, and the dram-drinking stranger was brought to decent moderation by the moral discrimination of Henry Lyon, Thomas Johnson and Mr. Jasper Crane, the next [tavern] licensee."

Lyon's main tavern clientele came from clusters of hamlets and farmhouses that sprang up in the Newark area. He made a fortune due to his "Scottish thrift, integrity and foresight. The ancestral habit of accumulating property was strong in him." Lyon's stature as an influential government official grew, and in December 1682, he was appointed the "commissioner to lay out highways, bridges, passages, landing and ferries for the County of Essex." Lyon, originally from Perthshire, Scotland (born around the year 1625), came to the colonies in 1648.[17] He first resided in Milford, Connecticut, and came to Newark as a founding member of the city. In later years, he moved to Elizabethtown, where he was a member of the general assembly. Lyon wrote a will dated February 9, 1702, and he died in Newark sometime between 1703 and 1707.

Author Charles H. Winfield documented the origins of Bergen, a village that was located in today's Jersey City, founded and organized by the Dutch between August and November 1660 and believed to be the first European settlement in the Garden State.[18] The village was laid out in a square, the sides of which were eight hundred feet long, and fortified by gates. "Streets quartered the town, and each quarter was divided into eight building plots," Winfield writes, adding that by May 1661, "not an unoccupied lot remained inside the fortifications. The buildings first erected were of logs."

The Dutch were skilled traders, craftsmen, brewers and distillers and had a fondness for juniper-flavored spirits, a cordial drink similar to British gin. Winfield writes that around the year 1664, within the village of Bergen, there were "many droughty [thirsty] burghers to whom a tavern could administer great consolation, [yet] there is no evidence that such an institution existed in the village [in these early years] by permission of the Dutch authorities."

Bergen did issue a license to a man named Christian Pietersen to "keep a hotel" in the village, which included the sale of alcoholic drinks "for the accommodation of strangers," declaring him to be "the fittest person for that employment." There's no mention of the year that Pietersen started his business, but Winfield states that Christian and "his good wife, Tryntje, continued to pass the pewter mug to all that was athirst until February 13, 1670, when his license was revoked and Hans Diedricks reigned in his stead." Another man named Hendrick Cornelisen "seems to have received a license March 10, 1669."

In 1668, a Frenchman named Peter Jegou obtained a permit from colonial governor Philip Carteret to "take up land on Leasy's Point on Burlington Island and…build and keep a house of entertainment for [the] accommodation of travelers."[19] Burlington Island is located on the Delaware River between Burlington and Bristol, Pennsylvania, on the New Jersey side of the river. Jegou obtained a license and "built a log house after the Swedish fashion. It was the only tavern in this part of the country. And it was well placed, for at this point the narrow footpath, which leads through the woods from the banks of the North River [and] comes out upon the Delaware."[20] Jegou and Henry Jacobs farmed on the island. Jegou also operated a tavern at Leasy's Point, just north of Burlington city. Robert Stacey, a Quaker, apparently coveted the island, and he later evicted Jegou and Jacobs. A book by historians Richard Veit and David Orr calls into question the legal standing of Jegou's permit from Carteret: "Our historical research indicates that Peter Jegou with Henry Jacobs were…at best, tenants of the governor and perhaps merely squatters."[21]

Middlesex County, on July 15, 1673, granted a license to Francis Drake to "keep an ordinary at New Piscataway."[22] Drake traced his ancestral roots to Devonshire, England, where he was born in 1615. He and his family came to America and lived in the Portsmouth, New Hampshire area. In April 1646, he was listed as part of a committee in Portsmouth regarding decisions on land use.[23] Drake; his wife, Mary; and three children (two sons and a daughter), all members of the Baptist faith, sold their land in New Hampshire and relocated to Piscataway in the 1660s to escape religious persecution. In 1665, New Jersey proprietors Lord John Berkeley and Sir George Carteret issued a "Concessions and Agreements" document, which guaranteed religious and personal freedoms and defined civic responsibilities and governmental structures.[24]

Drake and his family were among the early residents of New Piscataway. Around the same time he received his tavern license, the village appointed him as constable. He "was commissioned captain of the local militia [the Jersey Blues, serving from 1673 to 1685] and later he was successively justice of the peace and a member of the grand jury. Thus, Captain Francis Drake was prominent in the early annals of Piscataway." He died on October 23, 1687.[25]

Dr. Henry Greenland, relocating from New England, arrived as an early settler in Piscataway around 1675. Greenland accepted the position of captain of the Piscataway militia on July 27, 1675.[26] On November 16, 1679, Dutch missionaries Jasper Danckaerts and Petrus (Peter) Sluyter spent the night at Greenland's Piscataway residence, which Danckaerts described in his journal as a tavern (see "Wayfaring Strangers," in this chapter). Around 1680, Greenland moved to "King's Town" (Kingston) and built a house with a tavern near the King's Highway crossing of the Millstone River.[27] The proprietors of East and West New Jersey met at Greenland's Tavern in 1683 to decide on a common boundary. George

Greenland's Tavern, Kingston. *Photo by M. Gabriele.*

Keith, a prominent Quaker, surveyed the territory and established what became known as the "Keith Line," which separated East/West Jersey.[28] The proprietors returned to Greenland's tavern on January 8, 1687, and agreed to the terms of the Keith boundary line. "This survey was a major event of enduring practical significance for all New Jersey. It determined which province would control the granting of tens of thousands of acres of contested central New Jersey land."[29]

Author Elizabeth G.C. Menzies writes, "This was the bond of the proprietors of East and West Jersey given at their agreement to run the line of division betwixt the said provinces," noting that the meeting was held at Greenland's house/tavern overlooking the Millstone River—the present-day structure located at 1082 Kingston Road in Kingston.[30] The proprietors, in 1702, agreed to unite East/West Jersey as a single colony.[31]

The County Court of Middlesex County, which first met in Piscataway on June 19, 1683, weighed in on the importance of villages to maintain taverns. The court fixed taverns' rates for food, lodging and liquor. The court saw taverns as having value for the economic and social stability of a village, as well as serving the need for accommodations for travelers. "Each town was obliged by law as early as 1668 to keep an ordinary or tavern for relief and entertainment of strangers, under a penalty of forty shillings for each month's neglect. The innkeepers alone were permitted to retail liquors in quantities less than two gallons." Soon the court was being inundated with complaints of "great drunkenness in several towns, occasioned by persons selling liquor in private houses." Various laws were passed and then repealed. "The increase of punishment seems to have stimulated the vice, which may have been attributed to the removal of restrictions on the sale of liquors in small quantities."[32]

Henry Grubb received a license to keep a tavern in Burlington in 1681; his establishment was located near the Delaware River wharf at High Street. Burlington also issued a deed to Richard Basnett on February 20, 1685, as an innkeeper. The tavern was located at the intersection of High and Water Streets. Basnett died in 1694, and his widow, Elizabeth, continued to conduct the tavern, as Burlington meeting records make a reference to "Elizabeth Basnett's brewhouse."[33]

George Rescarrick, on December 17, 1700, purchased three hundred acres of land in Cranbury and won approval from proprietors to "keep a good house of entertainment for strangers and travelers." Rescarrick built a tavern in 1701 "at the junction on the north bank of the Cranbury Brook of Lawrie's Road from Perth Amboy and George's Road from New Brunswick." Post riders carrying mail from Perth Amboy to Burlington used Rescarrick's tavern as a midway rest stop. The tavern was a profitable enterprise, as Rescarrick's will, inventoried in 1720 after his death, "made ample provisions" for his wife, Mary; their children; and several associates. The family continued to run Rescarrick's Inn until the death of his son in 1729.[34]

WAYFARING STRANGERS

Colonial taverns welcomed weary travelers on their way to and from political, business, social and religious destinations. Their experiences at taverns became intertwined with their adventures. The writings of Benjamin Franklin and Jasper Danckaerts—two pilgrims traversing New Jersey's byways and waterways—have survived to provide firsthand observations of their travels. Their visits to colonial taverns sustained them on their respective journeys.

In 1723, Founding Father Benjamin Franklin, just seventeen years old, ambled through the wilds of the Garden State. As detailed in his autobiography, Franklin left his hometown of Boston in mid-September

1723 to escape the abuses inflicted on him by an overbearing older brother, with whom he was employed, and travel to New York City. As a young man, Franklin had been working as a printer and newspaper editor in Boston and believed there was employment to be had in Philadelphia. Franklin began his Garden State trek with a short stay in Perth Amboy on Tuesday, October 1, 1723.[35] It's plausible that Franklin spent the night at the Long Ferry Tavern in Perth Amboy, because the next day, he boarded a ferry and landed in South Amboy. Then he began his long walk, about fifty miles, to Burlington. There was a road between Perth Amboy and Burlington, which had opened in 1684.[36] In 1683, the New Jersey proprietors initiated a route "betwixt Perthtown (Perth Amboy) and Burlington," connected to a "ferry boat between Amboy and New York, to entertain travelers." However, these early colonial roads "were little more than foot paths, and so continued for many years, affording facilities to horsemen and pedestrians principally."[37]

On October 4, 1723, the young Mr. Franklin came upon a tavern in Bordentown, owned by Dr. Joseph Brown. It was a welcomed, much-needed stop, as Franklin wrote that he had been thoroughly soaked by a heavy rain and was

> *beginning now to wish that I had never left home. I cut so miserable a figure, too, that I found, by the questions asked me, I was suspected to be some runaway servant, and in danger of being taken up on that suspicion. I proceeded the next day, and got to an inn, within eight or ten miles of Burlington, kept by one Dr. Brown. He entered into conversation with me while I took some refreshment, and, finding I had read a little, became very sociable and friendly. Our acquaintance continued as long as he lived.*[38]

In his autobiography, Franklin writes that he spent the night at Dr. Brown's tavern and the next day, October 5, reached nearby Burlington, where he hoped to finish his journey with a boat ride to Philadelphia. Unfortunately, the regular ferryboats had left, with no service expected for at least three days, and he returned to the town, where he was befriended by a woman who offered him gingerbread. "She invited me to lodge at her house till a passage by water should offer, and being tired with my foot traveling, I accepted the invitation. She was very hospitable, gave me dinner of ox cheek with great good will."[39]

Burlington's Revell House, constructed in 1685, also known as the Gingerbread House, is where tradition says Franklin enjoyed his dish of ox cheek.[40] Thomas Revell, who worked as the clerk for the West Jersey

Above: Revell House, Burlington. *Photo courtesy of Jeff Macechak, Burlington County Historical Society.*

Right: Illustration of young Benjamin Franklin in Philadelphia. *From the collection of the New York Public Library.*

Assembly, purchased the home in 1696.[41] Originally located at the corner of Pearl and High Streets, not far from the Delaware River shoreline, it was moved to its current location on Wood Street in Burlington's London Historic District in 1966. The hearty meal at the Revell House apparently brought Franklin good luck. He went out for a walk along the Delaware River that same evening and happened on a boat with several people, bound for Philadelphia. He arrived there on Sunday, October 6, 1723, landing at the Market Street Wharf, and paid a visit to the Crooked Billet Tavern.

> *Walking down again toward the river, and looking in the faces of people, I met a young Quaker man, whose countenance I liked and, accosting him, requested he would tell me where a stranger could get lodging. We were then near the sign of the Three Mariners. Here, says he, "is one place that entertains strangers, but it is not a reputable house. If thee wilt walk with me, I'll show thee a better." He brought me to the Crooked Billet [Tavern] on Water Street. Here I got a dinner. After dinner, my sleepiness returned and, being shown to a bed, I laid down without undressing and slept till six in the evening; was called to supper, went to bed again very early, and slept soundly till next morning.[42]*

"Very Good Beer, Brewed by the Swedes"

Another wayfaring stranger, Jasper Danckaerts, a missionary from the Netherlands, kept a detailed journal of his travels with observations that provide a glimpse of daily life in seventeenth-century New Jersey—inside and outside of taverns. *The Journal of Jasper Danckaerts 1679–1680* was discovered in 1864 at a bookstore in Amsterdam.[43] Born in Zeeland, the Netherlands, on May 7, 1639, Danckaerts was a member of a Protestant religious sect known as the Labadists, a movement founded by a Frenchman, Jean de Labadie. In addition to his religious life, Danckaerts worked as a cooper (a maker of wooden casks, vats and barrels) for the Dutch West India Company. As recorded in Danckaerts's journal, he and his companion, Peter Sluyter, began their voyage to "New Netherland" on June 8, 1679, bound to New York from the Netherlands. They were on a mission for their Labadist community to establish a colony in the New World.

During his journey, Danckaerts recorded his stays at New Jersey taverns and elsewhere—hospitality that sustained the two men. The missionaries began their passage at the Dutch port town of Bolsward, arriving there via

Illustration of Pearl Street and Coentijs Slip, New York, 1679. *From the collection of the New York Public Library.*

a canalboat, on the morning of the religious holiday of Ascension Day, and their very first stop was a tavern. They reached New York in September 1679. Danckaerts wrote that he and Sluyter explored the city and were invited to be guests at the tavern of a local sheriff, "who had formerly lived in Brazil and whose heart was still full of it. This house was constantly filled with people, all the time drinking, for the most part that execrable [unpleasant] rum. He also had the best cider we have tasted."

Danckaerts and Sluyter soon gained passage to Staten Island. Friendly inhabitants of a plantation carried them by canoe to Mill Creek (possibly today's Elizabeth River), where they "determined to walk to Elizabethtown [Elizabeth]." On October 13, 1679, they arrived at a tavern kept by French papists.[44] From there, the two missionaries set off on October 22 and traveled by boat to Gamoenepaen (Communipaw) and then continued their journey "along a fine broad wagon road to a village called Bergen (Jersey City)... where the villagers, who are almost all Dutch, received us well." They traveled to Pescatteway (Piscataway) and reached the English village called

Wout Brigg (Woodbridge) on November 15, 1679. The next day, they spent the night at Greenland's tavern (mentioned earlier in this chapter).

> *We rode* [on horseback] *about two English miles through "Pescatteway" to the house of one Mr. Greenland, who kept a tavern there. We had to pass the night here, because it was the place of crossing the "Milstoone"* [Millstone] *River. Close by there, also, was the dwelling of some Indians, who were of service to this Mr. Greenland in many things. We were better lodged and entertained here, for we slept upon a good bed, and strengthened ourselves against the future.*[45]

Danckaerts and Sluyter enjoyed Greenland's tavern and mingled in a meeting of Quakers. "We tasted here, for the first time, peach brandy or spirits, which was very good, but would have been better if it had been more carefully made." They moved on, reached the Delaware River, continued to travel by boat and, on the evening of November 20, arrived at tavern in "Takany" (Tinicum Island, near Philadelphia). "Takany is a village of Swedes and Finns, situated on the west side of the river. We were well received and slept upon a parcel of deer skins. We drank very good beer here, brewed by the Swedes who, although they have come to America, have not left behind them their old customs."

Danckaerts and Sluyter continued heading south by boat and reached Maryland by December in order to fulfill their mission to locate a suitable tract of land to establish a Labadist community. In early January 1680, Danckaerts and Sluyter returned to New Jersey, having made arrangements to stay at the French tavern "which we have mentioned before, at Elizabethtown point," where they lodged for the night. "We were no sooner in the house [when] it began to rain and blow hard. We were therefore lucky in being housed. We had something left in our traveling sack, upon which we made our supper, and then laid ourselves down to sleep in our old fashion upon a little hay, before the fire."

The two Labadist missionaries returned to the Netherlands. Danckaerts's journal describes a second journey to America, in the spring and summer of 1683, returning to Maryland with the nucleus of a colony. Sluyter, who served as head of the colony, which numbered less than one hundred people, died in 1722. The Maryland community dissolved five years after his death. Danckaerts became a Maryland citizen in the early 1680s but returned to the Netherlands, where he died between 1702 and 1704. Jean de Labadie, the founder of the religious group, died in Germany in 1674.[46]

"This Inn Has Passed into Oblivion"

John Willis, a Philadelphia ship carpenter, purchased fifty acres of land in 1696 along the south side of Newton Creek, near Atmore's Dam, in what was then Gloucester County in West Jersey (today's Camden County). It was a perfect spot to build a tavern. The dam was the most convenient point to cross the creek, "a desirable stopping place, since the greatest number of folks could be seen in a given time. Being the head of navigation [near the Delaware River], all the trade carried on with Philadelphia by water in that neighborhood started from that point; a packet [boat] left every day for the city." Indian trails, some of which carved paths from the Delaware River to the Atlantic Ocean, surrounded the tavern. The inn became a place "where news from the city or country could be gathered, and whence correspondence could be forwarded to various parts of Gloucester and Salem counties."

The tavern—built partly of brick, with a hipped roof, small windows and a narrow door—had low ceilings, a large open fireplace and bright pewter dishes. Food was served in generous portions. The rustic menu included dried venison and bear meat, fish, wild fowl and cornbread. Alpha male patrons, as part of their rowdy entertainment, challenged each other to competitions of wrestling and running.

> *The visitors were mostly rude, uneducated people, unused to the refinements of society. At this old tavern might occasionally be seen a party of hunters, pledging their good opinion of each other in a bowl of whiskey punch or "stone fence" (a potent concoction of rum, cider, brandy or bourbon). The liquors, drawn from wooden casks and drank from horn tumblers, imparted an invigorating, healthy effect, and when evaporated by a good night's sleep, left no suspicious feeling after them.*

It's possible that the tavern might have stayed in business into the 1770s, operated by a series of innkeepers. Historian and author Judge John Clement of Haddonfield, writing in the 1870s, apparently relied on oral history sources and county lore to piece together the story of this lost tavern. Clement laments that most traces of this tavern have vanished, and the rough-hewn men who inhabited it, along with the tales they told, are long forgotten.

> *The Indian trails cannot be remembered by the oldest inhabitants. The name of this inn has passed into oblivion. Of this ancient house, not one stone rests upon another, as it stood in the days of our forefathers; and nothing*

but a slight depression in the ground shows its place. When this tavern at Atmore's Dam opened its doors to the public, or when it ended its days of usefulness, no record can be found; but like many other places of interest to the seeker of ancient things, enough has been gathered through tradition that deserves a faithful search, the more thoroughly to know its history. Around the broad, open fire of the barroom, the legends, the arguments or the songs will never be renewed.

Clement ends the chapter in his book with an excerpt from a melancholy eighteenth-century poem, "The Deserted Village," by Irish author Oliver Goldsmith, an elegy to the loss of a bygone era (*prest*: a Middle English word meaning "ready" or "prepared"):

Thither no more the peasant shall repair
To sweet oblivion of his daily care
No more the farmer's news, the barber's tale
No more the woodman's ballad shall prevail
No more the smith his dusky brow shall clear
Relax his ponderous strength, and lean to hear
The host himself no longer shall be found
Careful to see the mantling bliss go round
Nor the coy maid, half willing to be prest
Shall kiss the cup to pass it to the rest.[47]

CHAPTER 2

"THE ANTEDILUVIANS WERE ALL VERY SOBER"

"For the Entertainment of Travelers"

Taverns, inns, ordinaries, public houses and hostelries are terms describing a type of colonial establishment that provided alcoholic drinks, food and lodging. The names could mean different things to different communities. Some looked to capture the atmosphere of British pubs. The emphasis on particular services offered by a tavern depended on the establishment's ownership and regional needs, such as providing horse stables for stagecoaches. "The identity of the first public drinking and dining establishment [in the colonies] is obscure. It is certain, however, that it was known as an inn, tavern, or ordinary—names not always interchangeable. Tavern keeping has paralleled the growth of trade, travel, and industry throughout history and virtually worldwide. It is probable that taverns appeared in the United States almost as soon as the first Dutch settlers arrived."[48]

The oft-repeated phrase "for entertainment of travelers" would have referred to music, meals, drinks and games of chance as tavern entertainment. Establishing a tavern "was scarcely second to their providing a gathering place for the church," according to author Alice Morse Earle. "The early taverns were not opened wholly for the convenience of travelers; they were for the comfort of the townspeople, for the interchange of news and opinions, the sale of solacing liquors, and the incidental sociability; in fact, the importance of the tavern to its local neighbors was far greater than to travelers."

Tavern Scene, painting by David Teniers the Younger, 1658. *Courtesy of the National Gallery of Art, Washington, D.C.*

Morse Earle continues:

> *There was no putting on of airs or exclusiveness at Jersey taverns of the 1700s. Manners were rude even into the next century. All travelers sat at the same table. Frequently, the rooms were double bedded and four or more who were complete strangers often slept together. Anyone who objected to a stranger bedfellow was regarded as obnoxious and unreasonably fastidious. The landlord of colonial days may not have been the greatest man in town, but he was certainly the best-known, often the most popular, and ever the most picturesque and cheerful figure.*[49]

Charles S. Boyer gives a description of a tavern's warm welcome to guests:

> *Wherever there was a meeting house or church, there was, invariably, a tavern nearby. After a long ride through rain and snow, or under the fierce heat of a summer's day, the sight of a tavern was a welcome one to church goers. A stop was always made at its hospitable door, before going into the meeting and, under the influence of the refreshment at the bar and the*

roaring log fire, they were put in a more favorable mood to listen to the long, drawn-out sermon, returning at the conclusion of the services to fortify themselves either for the afternoon services or the drive homeward.[50]

ON THE ROAD

New Jersey taverns were stations on the colonial transportation network, which included ferry ports on the Delaware and Hudson Rivers, stagecoach routes and ancient Native American trails. This nascent colonial network outlined an early transportation blueprint for many of the state's roadways in the twentieth century, when New Jersey earned its designation as the Corridor State.[51] That title would have been equally appropriate for colonial New Jersey in the seventeenth and eighteenth centuries.

Thomas Fleming writes that, during the colonial years, a rudimentary transportation industry "took advantage of New Jersey's pivotal position between the two most dynamic American cities, New York and Philadelphia." The need to construct a transportation network to carry wood, furs, food and cash crops in a timely manner became a priority for colonial governments. "New Jersey got into the business of transporting people. By 1765 New Jersey probably had more roads than any other colony in British America; along [these roads] taverns multiplied amazingly. Well-located taverns soon became substantial affairs with large ballrooms, resident fiddlers for dancing, and innkeepers who were usually among the wealthiest and most influential men in the community."[52]

Burlington and Perth Amboy, as the respective capitals of West and East Jersey, established a stagecoach transit link in 1706, according to author George DeCou, who served as president of the Burlington County Historical Society in the first half of the twentieth century. He cites Burlington records that granted a license to Hugh Huddy on April 11, 1706, "for the transportation of goods and passengers" between Burlington and Perth Amboy. DeCou also transcribed an advertisement from the March 13–20, 1733 edition of the *American Weekly Mercury*, which reported that James Moon, a Burlington tavern owner, "keepeth two stage wagons intending to go from Burlington to Amboy" and back again, running on a weekly schedule. Moon also offered secure storage services for merchants' goods. Moon's tavern, known as Ye Olde Inn, stood at the corner of High and Broad Streets.[53]

This illustration by Isaac Weld (1774–1856) depicts a stage wagon leaving a tavern. *Courtesy of Lyuba Basin, Special Collections, J. Willard Marriott Library, University of Utah.*

> *Previous to 1675 and 1676, when the legislature adopted some general regulations for the opening of roads, the only road laid out by Europeans within the limits of New Jersey appears to have been that which the Dutch at New Amsterdam* [New York] *communicated with the settlements on the Delaware. It ran from Elizabethtown* [Elizabeth] *Point, or its neighborhood, to where New Brunswick now stands. At New Brunswick, the river was forded at low water, and the road thence ran almost in a straight line to the Delaware. In 1695 the innkeepers at Piscataway, Woodbridge and Elizabethtown were made subject to taxation to prevent* [the road from] *falling to decay.*[54]

This meant tavern owners, collectively, were on the hook to pay for road maintenance.

Kingston became a stagecoach stop during the mid-1700s.

> *Throughout the eighteenth century, the King's Highway, which runs through the center of Kingston, was the state's most-popular road for travel across New Jersey between Philadelphia and New York, and was the route for the*

colonial post riders and the New York–Philadelphia stagecoach lines. The road through Kingston was improved in 1765–1766, shortening the trip between Philadelphia and New York to only two days, so that Kingston and Princeton became centrally located for overnight stops.[55]

A popular spot in Kingston was Vantilburgh's tavern, "a favorite stopping place of Washington and the governors of New Jersey. It was at this village that Washington, with the American troops, eluded the British on the day of the battle of Princeton."[56]

The tavern of William Vantilburgh (also spelled Van Tilburgh) stood at the corner of today's Laurel Avenue and Main Street (Route 27), a site currently occupied by a restaurant. A colonial newspaper, dated June 1766, posted a sales notice that described "the old well-known tavern in Kingston, in Middlesex County, known by the Sign of the Mermaid, now in the possession of William Vantilburgh." The tavern had four fireplaces, a garden and a large stable and sat on a four-acre plot of land.[57] Vantilburgh's establishment achieved such renown that it earned a personal endorsement from President John Adams, who recommended it in a letter to his wife, Abigail, dated October 18, 1799. Adams wrote the letter during a stay in Trenton. "My dearest friend….If you have a mind to come nearer Philadelphia, you may find comfortable accommodations at Vantilburgh's at Kingston, where I can visit you every other day."[58] The tavern remained in the Vantilburgh family until it went out of business around 1880 and was demolished.

"Vantilburgh was a Patriot and his sons served in the local militia," George Luck Jr., treasurer of the Kingston Historical Society, said in a May 2022 interview. According to Luck, Vantilburgh received his license to operate the tavern in 1744 following petitions from village citizens.

Vincent Maresca and Ed Fox, interviewed in January 2021, are two men who know the lay of the land in the Garden State—both the current and ancient topography. Maresca serves as a historic preservation specialist in the Historic Preservation Office of the state's Department of Environmental Protection. Fox is a professional city planner and a consultant with an engineering environmental company in southern New Jersey. Both share a passion for understanding New Jersey's colonial roadways and how they've evolved over time. Both men noted that there were numerous "king's highways," "queen's highways," "York roads" and post roads throughout the state during the 1600s and 1700s. There were also "drover" roads where livestock could be "walked" to market. Maresca and Fox underlined the importance of taverns as stops on the expanding colonial road system, as well as their role in creating a social network among regions. A ten-mile segment of the old King's Highway received official designation in the National Register of Historic Places on October 23, 2000, encompassing Routes 27 and 206 in Mercer, Somerset and Middlesex Counties.[59]

Maresca said that waterways were the primary mode of transportation in the very early colonial years. As the population grew and villages were established, roadways opened up the state's interior and spurred commerce and settlement. Taverns were often found at crossroads at intervals to accommodate the needs of horses, Maresca said. Fox explained that, because ferries relied on a waterway's tidal schedule for the transport of ships, taverns at ferry slips were common as important places to entertain travelers as they waited out the clockwork of the tides. He said that beginning around 1704, the colonial governments appointed "overseers" (often tavern innkeepers) who were obligated to care for roads and waterways. From the 1730s to the 1760s, municipal offices were created to map and survey transportation routes. Fox said colonial roads typically "followed the wisdom" of Native American paths to avoid steep hills and swamps.

Charles S. Boyer writes that the first ferry slips "were primitive affairs, without waiting rooms for the accommodation of the public. In later years, rough board sheds were erected and provided with a stove in the middle of the room, around which the half-frozen ferrymen with their strong cigars or rank pipes would huddle."[60] Boyer writes that taverns near the river slips became a more pleasant refuge for travelers, who were compelled to wait (sometimes for extended hours or overnight) for the arrival or departure of ferries. "Most of the old highways in West Jersey either started from or ended at a tavern, a mill or a ferry. Because of the benefits to accrue to the tavern when a new road was laid out from or to it, the tavern keeper was assessed proportionally more than other property owners along its route."[61] Boyer writes that when the farmer or fisherman came to market with his load of farm produce or seafood, "these were taken across the river in baskets, and he had to have some place to leave his horse and wagon. By the time he had disposed of his wares, it was probably too late to start back home, and he would then return to the place where he had left his conveyance and stay [in a tavern] until early the next day."

Taverns were strategic points on military roadmaps. Robert Erskine, the official cartographer to George Washington, drew a map in 1777 for the Elizabethtown region (Linden and Rahway), which included the Wheatsheaf Tavern as a landmark.[62] The Wheatsheaf, originally known as the George Tavern, was built around the year 1730. The tavern, located near the intersection of Chestnut Street and Saint George's Avenue (Route 27) in Linden, was demolished in the fall of 1919 to make way for new road construction, presumably an expansion of Route 27.[63]

Travel by land during the colonial years presented numerous challenges. Colonial governments were well aware of these logistical problems, and so when they issued licenses for taverns, they typically included the proviso "for the accommodation and entertainment of travelers": in essence, a hospitality business. Government officials understood the practical issues concerning seventeenth- and eighteenth-century travel, which involved negotiating muddy, rocky roadways. Kym S. Rice writes that, during the colonial years, "the roads were terrible and travelers left accounts of journeys, which were tedious and disagreeable. A person did not have to be traveling a great distance to be in need of a tavern. Travel in colonial America was hazardous and fatiguing."[64] Fast-forward 250 years, and this commentary sounds painfully familiar for motorists navigating the Garden State Parkway during rush hour.

While driving a stage wagon along a bumpy, unforgiving colonial road, the sight of an eye-catching tavern sign might have enticed the driver to stop for his passengers to partake in refreshment or lodging. Tavern signs reflected a distinct kind of folk art of the period. Author David Steven Cohen writes that tavern sign illustrations "often took to the form of a rebus—an enigmatic representation of a word or phrase by pictures or symbols. People would meet 'under the sign of'; that is, at a certain tavern." Tavern signs, much like signs used to advertise other colonial trades, were designed to convey "the nature of the business at a time when many people could not read."[65]

Fraunces Tavern sign, New York City. *Photo by M. Gabriele.*

Tavern signs incorporated colonial folkcraft traditions of woodworking, painting and metalsmithing, according to Susan P. Schoelwer, PhD, executive director of historic preservation and collections for the Fred W. Smith National Library for the Study of George Washington at Mount Vernon, Virginia. "Signboards were painted on both sides and hung for maximum visibility, usually from a crossbar atop a high post or from a horizontal wooden bracket extending outward from the side of a house."

Schoelwer writes that the decorative imagery of tavern signs included horses, soldiers, ships, bulls, moons, suns, lions, eagles, grapevines, punchbowls and decanters. "The most sophisticated signs featured portraits, landscape compositions, or genre scenes, often adapted from print sources."[66]

A Physical Internet

"With the establishment of roads, inland taverns became essential," Marie Murphy Duess writes. "Larger towns were expected to have lodging for travelers. Taverns and inns were located at the crossing of two roads, and when possible, close to water. Respectable innkeepers were often influential in the town because they were constantly in touch with travelers, and could relate news of other localities (or gossip if they were so inclined)."[67]

Duess's narrative touches on the concept of the road as something more than just a route for transporting goods or moving people. The road during the colonial years also served as a conduit for sharing information—a physical Internet. Tavern owners collected descriptions of far-off places from their interaction with travelers—insights on the dynamics of colonial life. Stories were exchanged over glasses of rum, cider and beer, and no doubt these tales became more colossal and colorful as the conversations wore on. Tavern keepers became trusted "relayers of information," according to Kym S. Rice. "Travelers came to expect interrogations from their landlords and his or her clientele. Tavern keepers posted handbills, notices, and broadsides announcing sales, events, copies of colonial law and business transactions for the benefit of their customers."[68]

Steven M. Roth provides insight into the interdependence between taverns and the development of stage transport and improvement of colonial highways.

Although the carrying of freight initially provided the impetus for developing staging, in due course the carriage of passengers as a way of providing taverns and inns located along the stages' travel routes with a steady stream of customers proved to be the strongest motivating force. Carts and wagons replaced pack horses for the carriage of freight. To effectuate this, roads were widened and smoothed out, and plank surfaces added. Eventually, the wagons began to carry passengers as well as freight. As the number of passengers increased, staging...fell into the hands of innkeepers who catered to the needs of passengers, thereby providing themselves with a steady source of income for their taverns. Gradually, innkeepers bonded together to form stage lines with scheduled staging stops for meals and lodging. This became the pattern for future staging operations.[69]

Tavern owners were drawn into the delivery of mail—a disorganized and unreliable system.

Letters that went unclaimed were taken to a coffee house or a tavern that was heavily frequented by the community. The items were spread out on a table. People would come in and carried away not only their own letters, but all the letters belonging to people in the neighborhood. Most postmasters in major American villages and towns kept sloppy accounts or no accounts at all. The position was usually a part-time job financed by the Crown, given to the local customs official, printer, bookseller, tavern keepers, or simply anyone who was willing to do it. The colonists did not consider post officer or post rider a desirable position.[70]

The British Crown, in 1753, appointed Benjamin Franklin as postmaster general for the colonies. He surveyed colonial post roads and installed much-needed improvements to the mail system.[71]

Flying Machines

In May 1740, Joseph Borden, the founder of Bordentown, launched an integrated transportation system: a packet boat from the Crooked Billet Wharf in Philadelphia to Bordentown, accommodations for travelers in village taverns and then the Borden stagecoach, which drove to Perth Amboy, where passengers could make connections to New York via ferries. Doug Kiovsky of the Bordentown Historical Society explains that "by 1765, the Bordentown stage line was well patronized among individuals crossing the terrain of New Jersey. [Bordentown] presented its travelers with a fine array of stabled horses that complimented overnight accommodations that featured food and drink. Although packet boats along the Delaware River offered a safer and more leisurely alternative to the deplorable conditions of the terrain, there were many delays caused by changing tides and wind currents."[72]

The *Pennsylvania Gazette*, in its April 4, 1751 edition, outlined the Borden Stage route:[73]

Joseph Borden has a stage boat well fitted and, if wind and weather permit, will attend at the Crooked Billet Wharf in Philadelphia every Tuesday in every week, and proceed up to Bordentown on Wednesday, and on Thursday morning a stage wagon kept by Joseph Richards will proceed directly to John Cluck's opposite the City of Perth Amboy, who keeps a house of good entertainment, and on Friday morning a stage boat well fitted and kept by Daniel O'Bryant will proceed to New York and give her attendance at the White Hall slip near the Half Moon Tavern.

Stagecoach lines pitched their capabilities to overcome challenging road conditions, which ushered in the era of stagecoach "flying machines," so named to tout their promised speed for point-to-point service. The standard travel time for a trip between Philadelphia and New York was three days (including two tavern stops); the flying machines boasted that they could cut the travel time to two days. The Mercereau brothers, John and Joshua, were among the purveyors of this "flying machine" concept. They operated the Blazing Star Tavern on Staten Island and were entrepreneurs in the ferryboat and stagecoach businesses. The brothers posted an ad in the January 13, 1772 edition of the *New York Gazette or Weekly Post Boy*, outlining their services.[74]

The Flying Machine, kept by John Mercereau, at the new Blazing Star Ferry near New York, sets off from [Paulus Hook, Jersey City] *every Monday, Wednesday and Friday mornings for Philadelphia, and performs the journey in a day and a half for the summer season, till the first of November, from that time to go twice a week till the first of May. The wagons in Philadelphia set out from the* [George Tavern, at the corner or Arch and Second Streets] *the same morning.*

It would have been in the best interest of tavern owners and stagecoach operators to maintain a handshake alliance, as they complemented each other's businesses. In 1769, the Stage House Inn in Scotch Plains became a stop for the Swift Sure stagecoach line, which traveled from Philadelphia to New York. When a stagecoach arrived at the tavern with mail, the tavern staff fired miniature cannons, and townspeople dropped in to pick up their mail.[75]

George C. Pierson, genealogist and membership chair with the Historical Society of Scotch Plains and Fanwood and a former professor at Kean University, said in an August 2022 interview that original parts of the building date to 1737, when John Sutton, an early settler, turned his residence into

Stage House Tavern, Scotch Plains. *Photo by M. Gabriele.*

a tavern and inn. Since then, it's been known as Ye Old Historical Inn, Ye Olde Tavern, Sutton's Tavern and the Stanbery Inn; today, it is known as the Stage House Tavern.

The structure, still standing at the corner of Park Avenue and Front Street and operating as a restaurant, has been enlarged and remodeled over the years. Pierson said Continental army officers, including Major General Gilbert du Motier, the Marquis de Lafayette, met at the tavern to plan military strategy. Colonel Recompense Stanbery, one of the tavern's innkeepers, raised a liberty pole at the tavern in 1775, which became a gathering point for the Jersey Blues militia, as noted on the tavern's historic marker.

Read All About It

New Jersey's colonial taverns served as cozy reading dens, especially during the buildup to the Revolutionary War. Conversations involved the printed word—newspapers, mail and political pamphlets delivered by stagecoaches—along with firsthand oral accounts of timely events. By the 1770s, New Jersey taverngoers could read an assortment of newspapers, most of which were published in New York and Pennsylvania.

In the summer of 2009, the American Antiquarian Society, based in Worcester, Massachusetts, assembled an exhibition titled *A Place of Reading*. A tavern

> *was a place to gather, have a pint of stout, share a newspaper, peruse the latest broadside or pamphlet, and engage in friendly, or not so friendly, banter concerning the latest news. Newspapers were delivered by post to taverns, and the literate patrons eagerly read them aloud to their illiterate neighbors. In a time when news traveled slowly, all were eager for its arrival, literate or not. Time might stand still in the tavern, but things began to happen outside faster than many could grasp. News was vital, full of consequence and political. Are you a Loyalist or a Patriot? Do you support the English Crown or American independence? [Newspapers were] filled with sedition or freedom, depending on the reader's perspective. Taverns became breeding grounds for the Revolution. Reading was essential to the revolutionary process.*[76]

"Whether or not taverns were nurseries of the [colonial] legislatures, they were certainly seed beds of the Revolution, the places where British tyranny was condemned, militiamen organized, and independence plotted," according to W.J. Rorabaugh. "Patriots viewed public houses as the nurseries of freedom. The British called them public nuisances and the hot beds of sedition. There is no doubt that the success of the Revolution increased the prestige of drinking houses. A second effect of independence was that Americans perceived liberty from the Crown as somehow related to the freedom to down a few glasses of rum."[77]

Other historians cite the importance of taverns housing political discourse in the form of the printed word.

> *The ruling powers in England always had a jealous dread of the influence of the press, which in times of political excitement was wont to pour forth a torrent of virulent pamphlets. And so it was the rule to embody in the instructions given to the royal governors of the several provinces in America, strict injunctions for the restriction of the liberty of printing. As the Revolution progressed, the want of a newspaper in New Jersey that should reflect the sentiments of struggling Patriots was keenly felt.*[78]

Isaac Collins first published the *New Jersey Gazette*, the Garden State's first newspaper, on December 5, 1777. It was discontinued on November

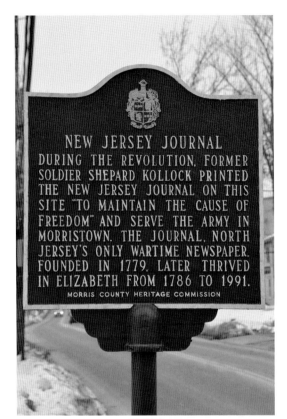

Left: Shepard Kollock historic marker, Chatham. *Photo by M. Gabriele.*

Below: Timothy Day's Tavern, Chatham. Drawing by Mary Keim Tietze. *Courtesy of the Chatham Historical Society.*

27, 1786. Collins's publication office was in Burlington and later moved to Trenton.[79] Shepard Kollock published the *New-Jersey Journal*, printed in Chatham, with the first edition dated February 16, 1779. Kollock worked as an apprentice for his uncle, William Goddard, a printer in Philadelphia, and became a colleague and friend of Isaac Collins. Kollock served as an artillery officer for the Continental army. He set up his first printing press in a back room of Timothy Day's Tavern. Day was a Patriot and endorsed the cause for "liberty, freedom and independence." Kollock's goal in printing the newspaper was to arouse support for the Patriots.

> *By the time Kollock's first issue came from his press, the Revolutionary War had long been underway, and the inhabitants of this little village [Chatham] of about twenty-four dwellings had become accustomed to changes in their former way of life. Chatham had become a point of great importance to the defense system of the Continental Army. Residents of the area had long been sympathetic to the Patriot cause, and a Liberty Pole, that symbol of non-conformity, had been raised in the village. Chatham was a strategic location for a newspaper. The town was of military importance; close to the enemy lines. [It] had a military hospital and was a beehive of Patriot activity.*

Sylvanus Seely, a Patriot militia colonel, farmer and tavern keeper, arrived in Chatham from Pennsylvania around 1772 and purchased a farm. A year later, Seely applied for a tavern license. Seely's tavern became Chatham's "link with the outside world." In 1775, Seely made a business arrangement for his tavern to become a regular stop for Constant Cooper's "complete and commodious stage-wagon," which had a route that connected Chatham with Newark, "Powles Hook" (Jersey City) and New York. Seely went to Timothy Day's tavern to watch the printing of the first edition of Kollock's newspaper.[80]

ALONG WITH STORIES ON issues of the day, eighteenth-century newspapers published detailed descriptions of taverns that were up for sale. These listings promoted the most attractive features of the businesses and often included an overview of a tavern's location (roadways and intersections with stagecoach stops). The tavern's adjoining property—the fields, crops, fruit trees and fresh, spring-fed streams—gave the business additional value and provided an indication of the type of food and drink that would be served.

These newspaper listings in the 1700s were advertisements, similar to real estate listings for homes and businesses found in current publications.

The May 6, 1771 edition of the *New York Gazette and Weekly Mercury* published a for-sale item on Campbell's Tavern in Freehold:[81]

> *The noted tavern in Freehold, known by the name of Campbell's Tavern, perhaps one of the best stands in* [Monmouth County], *with one-hundred acres of land, has a commodious house with four fireplaces and a good stable; also a good orchard of one hundred and fifty apple trees of the best sort, besides other fruit trees; a long railed garden with a prospect of five public roads, is situated within six miles of Middletown point and eleven* [miles] *of Amboy.*

On April 5, 1770, the *Pennsylvania Gazette* reported on a public "vendue" or auction, which was to take place on April 15.

> *The noted and well-accustomed tavern kept for many years by the subscriber, pleasantly situated in the center of Shrewsbury town, the English Church and Friends* [Quaker] *and Presbyterian meeting houses, two miles from a public landing, where there is a great commerce carried on from thence to*

Allen House Tavern, Shrewsbury. *Photo by M. Gabriele.*

New York. The house is very commodious, two stories high, [with] four fireplaces; a good dry cellar, large kitchen, a pantry or milk room, with many other out-houses and a shed and stable room enough for forty horses. [There is] a large garden, including half an acre of very rich land; a good bearing orchard that affords from thirty to 100 barrels of cider per year. An indisputable title will be given for the whole, and the conditions made known at the day of sale by Josiah Halstead.[82]

Halstead's tavern was built around 1680 and originally owned by a man named Judah Allen. Halstead purchased the business in 1754 from the Stillwell family and expanded the structure, which he dubbed the Blue Ball Tavern. The tavern, still standing and today known as the Allen House, was part of the "historic four corners" intersection in Shrewsbury, which included Christ Church, the Presbyterian Church and the Shrewsbury Religious Society of Friends (Quakers) meetinghouse and served as a town hall, post office and dance hall. Patriot/Loyalist disputes in the summer of 1779 led to a confrontation at the tavern. The incident, known as the Allen House Massacre, involved a group of Tories surprising Continental soldiers quartered at a tavern. A fight ensued, leaving three soldiers dead and others taken prisoner.[83] Today, the Allen House Tavern is maintained as a museum by the Monmouth County Historical Association.[84]

STRUCK BY JERSEY LIGHTNING

A whimsical 1745 poem by Benjamin Franklin, "The Antediluvians Were All Very Sober"—a nod to the ancient tribes living in the time before the Great Flood as described in the Bible—humorously refers to the widespread wisdom of the day: that much of the drinking water in the colonies was unsanitary, with stomach-churning bacteria, compared with safer, intoxicating libations.[85]

The Antediluvians were all very sober
For they had no wine, and they brew'd no October
All wicked, bad livers, on mischief still thinking
For there can't be good living where there is not good drinking.

'Twas honest old Noah first planted the vine,
And mended his morals by drinking its wine;

He justly the drinking of water decry'd
For he knew that all mankind, by drinking it, dy'd.

From this piece of history plainly we find
That water's good neither for body or mind
That virtue and safety in wine-bibbing's found
While all that drink water deserve to be drowned.

Kym S. Rice has identified rum (fermented and distilled from molasses, extracted from sugarcane) as a popular drink in eighteenth-century taverns.

The most expensive variety was imported from the West Indies; the rum of Jamaica was especially prized. Shipments to the Northeast from the islands began as early as 1670 and "northward" rum played a vital role in the development of the colonial economy. Before the Revolution, molasses and rum accounted for one-fifth of the value of all goods imported from British possessions. In 1770 the colonies alone imported four million gallons of rum and distilled another five million gallons. Plain [straight] rum was identified as the drink of the working classes.

Rum, fruit juices and spices became the ingredients for colonial punch, a favorite concoction among tavern customers.[86]

England's Caribbean sugarcane colonies, such as the island of Barbados, produced high-quality rum, but distillers in colonial New England started their own rum operations in the late seventeenth century. "The mainland colonies in North America took advantage of the growth and demand for the popular drink. American production of rum boomed as the colonies traded excess grains for molasses with Caribbean territories." The British attempted to impose restrictions and taxes on molasses, but "American colonial merchants flouted the regulations by smuggling cheaper molasses from French colonies."[87]

Along with rum, taverngoers had an affinity for alcoholic apple cider. Apples for Newark cider were harvested in fields located in sections of today's Bloomfield.

The farmers raised on the land rye, oats, Indian corn, potatoes and buckwheat, wheat, and hay. They had large orchards of apples for making cider, which, under the name of "Newark cider," was known over a large extent of the country. It was celebrated as the best. It was made from two kinds of apples mixed: two-thirds being Harrison apples…and one-third being the Campfield apple. Thus, Newark cider was a product of Newark fruit and Newark invention.[88]

The Granniwinkle and Poveshon were two other varieties used for the production of Newark cider.[89]

Laird and Company, located in the Monmouth County town of Scobeyville, is a source of New Jersey pride as the oldest family-owned licensed distillery in the United States. Lisa Laird Dunn, the ninth-generation owner of the operation, interviewed in November 2020, said her ancestor William Laird traveled to colonial New Jersey in 1698 from County Fife in Scotland, near Edinburgh. According to her family's oral history, William came to the New World in order to escape the persecution being suffered by Scottish clans.

Laird Dunn said her family has been a producer of apple brandy in New Jersey since the early 1700s and that the first written sales records are from the year 1780. Family lore indicates that George Washington was a fan of Laird's apple brandy—so much so that sometime in the late 1750s, he wrote a letter to Robert Laird, another family ancestor, requesting the secret family recipe. Laird Dunn confirmed that Robert did share the recipe but added that, unfortunately, the letter written by Washington has been lost. The time frame for the letter seems to coincide with two terse diary entries by Washington in 1760.[90] On February 26, 1760, Washington noted that his farm in Mount Vernon, Virginia, had "bottled thirty-five

Laird and Company sign, Scobeyville. *Photo by M. Gabriele.*

dozen of '*cyder*'; the weather very warm and cloudy, with some rain last night." On March 1, 1760, he wrote that the farm had "finished bottling ninety-one dozen of cyder."

Apple cider is a precursor to distilled apple brandy, Laird Dunn explained. Apples are pressed, and the juice is fermented. During the colonial period, freezing or "jacking" the juice in wooden casks during the winter months was a common method of distillation. The cold-weather jacking would separate the excess cider-water ice from the alcohol, leaving behind a condensed, potent brandy.

Along with its production of spirits, the Laird family once operated the historic Colt's Neck Tavern, which dates to the year 1717. Laird's applejack brandy is the renowned flagship brand of the family business and became a bestseller in New Jersey's colonial taverns. Robert Laird served as a soldier under Washington, and the family's history indicates that he generously provided applejack to the troops passing through Monmouth County during the war. This product also garnered a catchy nickname: Jersey Lightning.

George's Small Beer Recipe

Beer had its place as a healthful beverage during the colonial era. Colonial brewers cracked malted barley by hand and then soaked the grains in boiling water, a process they called mashing, which extracted sugars from the barley. Brewers dumped the mash, which had the consistency of oatmeal, into a whiskey barrel. The barrel acted like a sieve, filtering the liquid from the grain. The strained liquid (called wort) went into a copper pot and boiled for two hours. The brewer then chilled the liquid, added hops, sprinkled it with yeast and drained the final product into wooden kegs, which were allowed to age for about a month. "Beer was essential to a good diet. Although no one realized it at the time, the beer-making fermentation process cleansed the otherwise fetid water, killing pathogenic micro-organisms and even provided nourishment."[91]

The *Journal of the Institute of Brewing* points out that "beer is intrinsically resistant to the growth of spoilage and pathogenic (disease-causing) microorganisms, owing to a combination of inhibitory factors. Many stages of the brewing process reduce the potential for contamination or the proliferation of bacteria."[92] Pumpkins often topped the list of colonial "fermentables" used to fortify and flavor the brewed wort.

Pumpkins grew wild in the colonies and, when blended with malt, pumpkin starches could easily be broken down into sugars in a mash. Colonial brewers also used molasses, peaches, persimmons, Jerusalem artichokes, peas, corn stalks, along with spruce, used as a flavoring and preservative. The business incentive to produce beer in the colonies was great. Beer imported from England took up valuable space aboard ships, and often was not fit to drink after voyages lasting months, under less-than-optimal storage conditions.[93]

A Dutchman named Aert Teunissen Van Putten (or Aert Teunissen of Putten, the Netherlands, a town located forty miles east of Amsterdam), might have been the first person to brew a batch of beer in New Jersey. Van Putten was among the earliest settlers in Hoboken.

On the 15th of February, 1640, Governor [Willem] Kieft leased land in Hoboken to Aert Teunissen Van Putten for twelve years. Kieft agreed to erect a small house.…There is no doubt that the house which Kieft built for Teunissen was the first building in Hoboken. Teunissen forthwith began to improve his leasehold. He cleared the lands, fenced the fields and erected a brew house. Thus he became the first brewer within [Hudson] county, if not within the state. He stocked his farm with twenty-eight head of large cattle, besides various small stock such as swine, goats and sheep, along with many fruit trees.[94]

Teunissen was killed during a trading expedition near Sandy Hook in 1643.[95] It's believed that the brewhouse stood until 1645.[96] Teunissen's farm was part of a plantation system that spanned the village of Bergen (today's Jersey City) and Hoboken. The plantation environs "constituted a thriving settlement," suggesting Teunissen would have had ample customers for his beer.[97]

Similar to the growth of today's craft beer business and brewpubs throughout the Garden State, colonial brewing became a popular artisan profession. A lively brewery scene percolated in Burlington on West Pearl Street in the late seventeenth century. This street provided brewers with easy access to the Delaware River waterfront. Beer brewing "factored in both business relations with Philadelphia and its products in trade with the Caribbean." By the late 1670s, "incoming ships had elevated Burlington's population to approximately eight hundred settlers, which made the brewery's wharf district bustle with maritime and economic activity. Burlington became a port with constant presence of tall-mast ships in its harbor. The

Brew House, Burlington. *Photo courtesy of Jeff Macechak, Burlington County Historical Society.*

wharf neighborhood employed ship chandlers, coopers, brewers, carpenters, blacksmiths, bakers, potters, maltsters, tanners, butchers, tavern keepers and sail-makers."[98]

Prominent brewers included Thomas Budd, who came to Burlington from Somersetshire, England, with his family in 1678. Budd owned a tavern and brewery. "He likely built his brick tavern at the corner of High and Pearl streets, and the structures devoted to the manufacture of beer. A granary extended from the rear of the tavern. A malt house and brew house stood behind the tavern. In 1693 Thomas Budd sold his Burlington property, including the brewery, to Samuel Jenkins."[99]

In 1685, Budd published a booklet in which he described the agricultural abundance of the region in and around Burlington to support the brewing trade and the tavern business.[100] The land, he wrote, "would bear great crops of wheat, [peas], barley, hemp and flax, and it would be very fit for hop gardens. The water is clear, fresh and fit for brewing. The air is clean and good." Budd saw business opportunities to be exploited in this idyllic setting.

> *I do not question but that we might make good, strong, sound beer, ale and mum* [a special ale brewed from wheat and bitter herbs] *that would keep well to Barbados, the water being good, and wheat and barley in a few years* [likely] *to very plentiful. Great quantities of beer, ale and mum are sent yearly from London and other places, to Barbados, Jamaica and other islands in America, where it sells to good advantage. If merchants can gain by sending beer, ale and mum from England, where corn is dear and freight is dear, by reason of the length of the voyage, we in all probability must get much more.*

Budd also envisioned profitable ventures in harvesting fruit for the production of other alcoholic beverages. "Orchards of apples, pears, quinces, peaches, [apricots], plums, cherries and other sorts of the usual fruits of England may soon be raised to good advantages. The trees [grow] faster than in England, whereof great quantities of [cider] may be made. It is supposed that we may make good wines as in France…for the climate is as proper as any part of France."

As mentioned in the introduction of this book, New Jersey's provincial congress met in Burlington in the summer of 1776 at the Blue Anchor Tavern, which was located at the corner of High and Broad Streets and built around 1750, two stories in height. "At the time of the Revolutionary War, when James Edsall was 'mine host,' the Blue Anchor was at the height of its glory. It was the leading tavern in Burlington." The rebellious provincial congress adopted a new constitution for New Jersey on July 2, 1776. Congress members also called for the arrest of Governor William Franklin, the son of Founding Father Ben Franklin and the last "royal" governor of the state. Political unrest began brewing in Burlington in the mid-1760s, and taverns there welcomed "aroused colonists criticizing their king, merchants voicing protests over harsh British trade restrictions, and travelers bearing news of similar ferment in other colonies. It was in taverns that petitions were drawn up and signed, tea boycotts organized and militia groups formed." Some Burlington residents didn't support independence aspirations, including then-mayor John Lawrence, "an ardent Tory who later ceremoniously welcomed British and Hessian officers, but whose door was closed to Patriot legislators." Burlington's taverns kept their doors open to the Patriots. Edsall was sympathetic to the revolutionary cause, and the Blue Anchor housed local political leaders who held all-night debates in the taproom and secret committee sessions in the tavern's parlor.[101]

Authors Harry B. and Grace M. Weiss recount the story of how brothers John and Andrew Thompson, along with their families, set sail from Dublin, Ireland, in September 1677 and landed in December at Elsinboro Point, a village on the Delaware River, four miles west of Salem. As members of John Fenwick's Salem Quaker colony, they farmed and brewed beer beginning in 1680, a profitable enterprise that had customers in Philadelphia and New York.

Harry and Grace Weiss transcribed a sales notice published in the September 15, 1748 edition of the *Pennsylvania Gazette*, which provided details of a brewery in Bordentown.

> *In West New Jersey and the county of Burlington in the township of Chesterfield, there is to be sold a good malt house made of brick work and a brew house, joining together, with copper tubs, coolers, malt mills, spouts and pumps, all convenient for the brewing of good beer, situate*[d] *at Bordentown, on a large wharf upon the river Delaware, which is so convenient that you may lower your beer with a tackle into the boats or shallops* [a one-mast river barge designed for carrying heavy cargos], *which are passing almost every day either to Philadelphia, Burlington or Trenton.*

Harry and Grace Weiss also note the changing times, tastes and the business climate for alcohol consumption in western New Jersey: "Before 1790 there were several well-built brick buildings erected [in Salem County] for the manufacture of beer for the early settlers. Later generations of settlers planted apple orchards. And when these came into bearing, the fruit was used for cider and apple brandy, which together with rum from the West Indies, gradually displaced malt liquors."[102]

The New York Public Library preserves a handwritten beer recipe from George Washington, which he entered into his notebook in 1757, while he was stationed at Fort Loudon, Pennsylvania, serving as a colonel of the Virginia militia during the French and Indian War.[103] It has been described as a formula for "small beer…notable for its low alcohol content." The recipe's inclusion in Washington's wartime notebook suggests that this beer was consumed as a regular beverage and even perhaps an occasional substitute for water among his troops. "The recipe is succinct, requires very few ingredients, and has a remarkably short preparation time of little more than a day." The recipe reads:[104]

> *To Make Small Beer:*
> *Take a large siffer* [sifter] *full of bran; hops to your taste. Boil these three hours, then strain out thirty gallons* [for] *three hours into a cooler. Put in three gallons* [of] *molasses while the beer is scalding hot, or rather draw the molasses into the cooler and strain the beer on it while boiling hot. Let this stand till it is little more than blood warm, then put in a quart of yeast. If the weather is very cold, cover it over with a blanket and let it work in the cooler twenty-four hours, then put it into the cask. Leave the bung open till it is almost done working. Bottle it that day/week it was brewed.*

It's refreshing to know that, along with his many military responsibilities, the Father of Our Country found time to take a break and jot down a simple beer recipe in his notebook.

The Ballad of Elizabeth Haddon

"A sizable book of the greatest historic and human interest could be written about the Quaker lady who founded the village of Haddonfield and whose maiden surname was given to that locality in old Gloucester County long before the village of Haddonfield was thought of." Historian Frank H. Stewart is praising Elizabeth Haddon, who was born in the London borough of Southwark in 1680 and came to the New Jersey colony in 1701.[105] Her mission was to oversee the development of a large tract of land in present-day Haddonfield, purchased by her wealthy British father, John Haddon. This was a long-distance transaction; John Haddon never visited New Jersey. Elizabeth served as his representative. The property was designated as a plantation that eventually included a mansion and a brick brewhouse.

When she arrived in West Jersey, Haddon faced formidable challenges to establish the Haddon plantation in a remote wilderness, according to

Stewart. "There were probably not more than two or three dwellings on the main street of the present town, and they of the most primitive sort—a tavern, a blacksmith shop, a log cabin or two at magnificent distances. In short, the town of Haddonfield was not on the map."

Haddon relied on a network of Quaker families in West New Jersey to achieve her goals. Author Jeffery M. Dorwart, in a May 2021 email exchange, stated that "Elizabeth would immediately fit into the women's Friends weekly meetings and these women all helped each other." Dorwart, professor emeritus of history at Rutgers University, and his coauthor, Elizabeth A. Lyons, write that when Elizabeth Haddon arrived in West New Jersey at the age of twenty-one in the spring of 1701 (she endured the six-week sea voyage and initially landed in Philadelphia), she found herself in an environment of swamps, woodlands and creeks inhabited by "the Algonquin-speaking Lenape Native American peoples." Elizabeth "found many strong, independent Quaker women present in West New Jersey" and enjoyed the support of the Quaker community through her marriage to Quaker missionary John Estaugh on December 15, 1702.

Between 1705 and 1708, Haddon made plans to establish the plantation and a brewhouse. The plantation had two stills and produced hard cider and wine. "I'm not sure how large the Estaugh's brewery was, but it did sell

Elizabeth Haddon's distillery house, Haddonfield, circa 1938. *Courtesy of Joanne M. Nestor, New Jersey State Archives, New Jersey Department of State.*

hard cider and probably beers," Dorwart said. A letter written by Haddon's father indicated he had shipped his daughter two hundred bottles of a highly alcoholic concoction of macerated roots of herbs and spices known as bitters, presumably for medicinal purposes. Dorwart referenced minutes from the February 12, 1722 Haddonfield Monthly Meeting of Friends, which reported that the first gathering "in our new meeting house in Haddonfield was held on February 12, 1722." The "hospitalities" would have included Haddon's cider and wine and the alcoholic bitters. The meetinghouse proved to be a magnet to attract new people to the growing community. "Soon new Quaker shopkeepers, innkeepers, craftsmen, landowners, and visitors from Philadelphia and other parts of the Delaware Valley found their way to settle, work and trade in Haddonfield."[106]

Quaker historian Samuel N. Rhoads compiled a history of Elizabeth Haddon and presented a paper, "Haddon Hall of Haddonfield," to the Friends' Historical Society of Philadelphia on January 25, 1909. Rhoads described a "spacious" underground vault that straddled the mansion and the brewhouse.

> *No doubt* [the vault] *was well stocked with liquid refreshment, tonic beverages and medical potions in those earlier days when Haddon Hall was in the heyday of its reputation as a sort of half-way house between Burlington and Salem's yearly meetings and Philadelphia....A search among the journals of traveling ministers of the period shows that Haddon Hall had almost a monopoly in the hospitalities given to public Friends visiting the neighborhood.*[107]

John Estaugh died on December 6, 1742, on the Caribbean island of Tortola during a missionary expedition. By 1760, Elizabeth had grown weary from illness and advancing years. She died on May 30, 1762, and was buried in the Haddonfield Friends Burial Grounds, near her plantation residence.

Haddonfield's House of Hugh Creighton (described in the introduction), today known as the Indian King Tavern, served as a meeting place for New Jersey's general assembly, where legislators declared New Jersey to be a state and not a colony. Matthias Aspden, a Philadelphia merchant, erected the structure in 1750. The building was expanded in 1764 and purchased by Thomas Redman in 1775. Redman sold the property to Hugh Creighton in May 1777, and he established the site as a tavern. Michelle Hughes, the resource interpretive specialist at the Indian King Tavern, said in an interview that by 1777, Haddonfield had evolved into a farming village and economic center in southwestern New Jersey. Today, the tavern operates as a public museum under the management of New Jersey's Park Service within the Division of Parks and Forestry.[108]

Letitia G. Colombi, the first female mayor of Haddonfield, reflected on her ascent to public office as being connected to Elizabeth Haddon's legacy. Colombi served for twenty-two years as a Haddonfield commissioner, including twelve years as mayor. "Elizabeth Haddon is beloved by our residents," Colombi said in a January 2022 interview. "She was a leader and left us with a wonderful history. She made Haddonfield a place to welcome people." When asked what Colombi might say if she could magically go back in time to meet Haddon, she replied: "I would say thank you for your inspiration. I hope we've made you proud."

WOMEN TAVERN OWNERS

Many women assumed the economic responsibility of running family taverns and other businesses in the absence or after the death of their husbands. Compared with men, married women held an inferior legal status in colonial society.

From the early decades of the seventeenth century, women emigrated from Holland, Sweden, England, Germany, Ireland and Scotland, envisioning opportunities of prosperity and well-being in the New World. The life of women in the colony reflected colonial society at large, combined with the particular features of the New Jersey settlement. They labored as worker companions with their spouses and followed a sexual division of labor conventional in an agricultural society. The legal and property rights of women in New Jersey came under English common law. A married woman…surrendered control of property to her husband. Wages earned by a married woman legally belonged to her husband. By contrast, single women and widows worked in trades and other occupations, such as tavern keepers, out of necessity. Unmarried women were permitted to own property and form businesses, but they typically were discounted as being objects of pity.[109]

On February 11, 1735, the mayor, recorder and aldermen of New Brunswick met at the House of Ann Balding to pass a street-paving ordinance. City records show that on December 24, 1735, Balding received

Reenactors from the Second New Jersey Regiment, Helm's Company, pose at Dey Mansion Washington's Headquarters, Wayne. *Photo by M. Gabriele.*

a note of payment for entertaining the lawmakers. The tavern might have been located near the intersection of Commercial Avenue (Paul Robeson Boulevard) and Burnet Street. New Brunswick council records posted in February 1743 refer to Ann as the "widow Balding." Her husband, tavern owner John Balding, captained two sloops and presumably was lost at sea around 1742.[110]

Sarah Badgley twice inherited the Sign of the Unicorn Tavern in Elizabethtown (Elizabeth) following the deaths of two husbands. John Clark established the tavern around 1760 and married Sarah. The tavern, which was located on the corner of today's Broad and East Jersey Streets, became popular due to its location as a stagecoach stop. In addition to being a favorite place for local residents, the tavern featured a "long room" that held community meetings and special municipal/legal proceedings. John Clark died in 1771, leaving Sarah to carry on the business, and she did so successfully. Two years later, she married William Graham, a village tailor described as a frequent, loyal patron of the tavern.[111]

Following the marriage of Sarah and William, the establishment came to be known as Graham's Tavern. An essay described the atmosphere of the house.[112]

There were rooms of generous proportions, located on the second floor, where fair-sized assemblages could be held. Many a happy gathering convened at William Graham's long room. It was not unusual in the evening, after early candle light, to hear the sweet strains of harps and fiddles, while belles and beaux danced the stately minuet. The roaring fires in the grates, the sounds of laughter and the swish of satin [dresses] as the dancers went through the graceful figures, brought life into the scene. The minuet was usually followed by reels and cotillions, and finally the Virginia reel.

William Graham died in 1779, once again leaving the responsibility of tavern management to Sarah. At this point, perhaps faced with financial difficulties, she decided to sell off interior appointments of the tavern. She placed an advertisement in the March 23, 1779 edition of the *New Jersey Journal*, which listed beds, tables, desks, decanters and glasses to be sold at a public vendue the following month. Sarah married a third time and turned over tavern ownership to family members. She died in 1793.

Author Frank H. Stewart lauds Ann Risley as "the queen of all, whose tavern [in Absecon] was known far and wide for its generous and gracious hospitality. The fish, clams, oysters and crabs of Little Egg Harbor Bay and its tributaries, not to say anything of the sugar, molasses and rum from the West Indies, made the tavern of Ann Risley known all over the province."[113] Stewart recorded the application by Risley's bondsmen for an April 10, 1770 tavern license renewal, which read:

To the honorable bench of the justices assembled at Gloucester: The humble petition of Ann Risley, widow of Great Egg Harbor Township [then part of Gloucester County], *in the province of West New Jersey, humbly sheweth that your petitioner, having kept a tavern near Abesekom Bridge in the said township for several years past, hath thought proper to acquaint your honors that she hath built her house with stabling and other conveniences for the entertainment of travelers, thereby doth humbly entreat your honors to grant her a license to continue the same, it being a suitable stage, there being no other within ten miles and in vindication of the truth of this likewise of her character, several of the principal inhabitants of said province have thought proper to set their hand hereunto. Your honors taking the same into consideration will oblige your petitioner to ever pray—Ann Risley.*

This petition identified Ann as a widow. In 1762, the county issued a tavern license to Peter Risley, Ann's husband. Peter died sometime after

1762, and Ann carried on with the business, receiving her own tavern license in 1767. Authors Sarah W.R. Ewing and Robert McMullin note that early inns and taverns "were the cynosure [center of attention] for all eyes in the village, and Ann Risley's inn was no exception. She had a public vendue in her tavern on May 29, 1771 when Samuel Smallwood, High Sheriff, sold five hundred fifty acres, 'late the estate of Joseph Adams, deceased.'" Risley's tavern was the site of community meetings, legal notices, sheriff sales, government proclamations, mail deliveries and stagecoach arrivals and departures.[114]

An advertisement in the March 24, 1773 *Pennsylvania Journal* mentioned Risley's establishment: "Going from Great Egg Harbor to Philadelphia once every week to set off from Ann Risley's [tavern] on Monday morning." Stagecoach operations began in 1773 between Samuel Cooper's Ferry in Camden and Absecon. The route may have been the precursor for today's White Horse Pike (Route 30). Stagecoaches "left Ann Risley's Tavern on Monday mornings," traveled through present-day Port Republic and Haddonfield and arrived at Cooper's Ferry the following afternoon.[115] The fame of Risley's tavern died with her, and another license wasn't issued in the village for ten years, according to Ewing and McMullin. Risley wrote a will, dated November 26, 1781, and died around 1787.

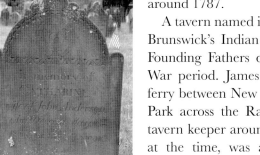

Gravestone of Catharine Anderson (1749–1806). She and her husband, John, managed the Rahway Community House, known today as Merchants and Drovers Tavern, in Rahway. *Photo by M. Gabriele.*

A tavern named in the female gender, New Brunswick's Indian Queen, received several Founding Fathers during the Revolutionary War period. James Drake, who operated a ferry between New Brunswick and Highland Park across the Raritan River, became the tavern keeper around 1778. New Brunswick, at the time, was a prosperous river port. Located at the corner of Albany and Water Streets, it's believed the two-story building originally was constructed in the early 1700s as a private residence prior to becoming a tavern, using locally excavated brownstone for its walls.[116]

Drake marketed his ownership of the tavern in an advertisement in the October 20, 1783 edition of the *Guardian*, a New Brunswick newspaper. He pledged to accommodate

Merchants and Drovers Tavern, Rahway. *Photo by M. Gabriele.*

"gentlemen and ladies to the best of his abilities." On September 9, 1776, the tavern hosted Benjamin Franklin and John Adams, who were traveling through the region on their way to Staten Island.[117] The two luminaries were forced to share a single room and disagreed over whether to leave the

Indian Queen Tavern interior, East Jersey Old Town. *Photo by M. Gabriele.*

window opened or closed before turning in for the night. (Adams was the one who wanted it closed.) No doubt they also disagreed over who snored the loudest. This episode in New Brunswick occurred just two days before Adams, Franklin and Edward Rutledge met with Lord Richard Howe, representing the British Crown, at Colonel Christopher Billopp's estate on Staten Island (later known as the Conference House), in a failed attempt to avoid war and negotiate independence for the colonies.[118]

Another newspaper article, dated December 9, 1783, reported on a grand reception at "Mr. Drake's tavern," organized by New Brunswick dignitaries to honor George Washington and Baron Friedrich Wilhelm Augustus von Steuben, who were passing through New Brunswick. Baron von Steuben was a military officer from Prussia, credited with instilling discipline in Continental army soldiers. The affair at Drake's tavern celebrated the September 3, 1783 signing of the Treaty of Paris, the document that officially ended the Revolutionary War. Glasses were raised for thirteen toasts, apparently symbolizing the thirteen colonies now transformed into states. Flush with patriotic optimism, one of the toasts offered hope that "the American Revolution be propitious to the cause of freedom throughout the world."

The tavern survived as a historic structure until the 1970s. A Route 18 road-expansion project threatened to demolish the structure, but it was moved, reassembled and reopened in 2005 as part of Piscataway's East

Jersey Olde Town village—an outdoor collection of vintage buildings relocated to Johnson Park, maintained by Middlesex County's Board of Chosen Freeholders, Cultural and Heritage Commission and Department of Parks and Recreation. According to an article in the fall 2005 edition of the *Link*, a newsletter published by the Raritan Millstone Heritage Alliance, Dr. Joseph Kler, a historian and philanthropist, along with his wife, Elizabeth, and daughter Marjorie, in 1971, led the initiative to save the Indian Queen. Marjorie served as a regent of the Jersey Blue Chapter of the Daughters of the American Revolution and worked as the director and curator of the village. Joseph, and later Marjorie, served as presidents of East Jersey Olde Town.[119]

An archaeological dig (part of the "Route 18/27 Albany Street Interchange Site") conducted in 2003, adjacent to the Raritan River, uncovered the foundation of the Indian Queen along with artifacts such as shards of platters, oyster shells, nuts, peach and cherry pits and, most curiously, a fragment of a coconut shell, all of which are on display at the tavern museum.

JOHN DICKINSON'S GREATEST HIT

The sound of the fiddle filled New Jersey's colonial taverns as patrons drank merrily and sang songs from their homelands. The fiddle was the dominant instrument used for performing in eighteenth-century taverns, but in some conservative colonial religious circles, fiddle playing and dancing carried a shameful stigma. Laws were enacted to forbid secular merriment in public or in taverns, especially on the Sabbath. Music was singled out as an activity that inspired rowdiness and promiscuousness.[120] The General Assembly of East New Jersey met in Elizabethtown and Woodbridge between October 10 and 13, 1677, to produce an edict stating:

> *Be it enacted by this Assembly that…any person or persons misbehaving themselves, namely staggering, drinking, cursing, swearing, quarreling or singing any vain songs or tunes of the same, shall cause the said person or persons so offending to be set in the stocks for two whole hours without relief.*

Charles S. Boyer says there were two classes of taverns in New Jersey during the pre– and post–Revolutionary War years: one for "the accommodation of stagecoach and private travelers; and the other class where wagoners, teamsters and drivers 'put up' [for the night]."[121] John Omwake writes:

Merrymakers in an Inn (1674), painting by Adriaen van Ostade (1610–1684). *Public domain.*

Wagoners were a noisy, jolly crew who loved to frolic and dance. At the end of the day, when the horses stood eating contentedly under the stars, and their bells were silent, the music of the violin usually was heard inside the tavern, and the wagoners, who had walked probably the greater part of the twenty miles that their teams had traveled that day, danced to whatever tune the fiddle sang: the Virginia Reel, the French Reel, Four Square, Jim Crow or Hoe Down, and for refreshments there was "Monongahela" [whiskey] at three cents a glass.[122]

Above: Musicians Ridley and Anne Enslow performing on fiddle and hammer dulcimer at East Jersey Old Town. *Photo by M. Gabriele.*

Left: The *Boston Chronicle* newspaper, August 29– September 5, 1768. *Courtesy of Malinda Triller-Doran, Special Collections Librarian, Dickinson College, Carlisle, Pennsylvania.*

The Genealogy of the Bonnell Family, a privately published manuscript from the late 1800s, describes the Old Revolutionary Inn in the village of Hunt's Mills (present-day Clinton), which was established in 1767 by Colonel Abraham Bonnell, a Revolutionary War hero. Tavern regulars who gathered around the tavern's hearth during the evening hours included "the usual group of uncouth figures…famed gossips that smoked, drank and sang many a good song, which made the walls ring on these genial, convivial occasions." The historic structure, today known as Bonnell's Tavern, still stands in Hunterdon County and is being rebuilt by Henry Bonnell, a direct descendent of Colonel Bonnell (see the Bonnell's Tavern section in chapter 4).

Founding Father John Dickinson (1732–1808), a scholar, political leader and author during the Independence movement, composed the anthem "The Liberty Song," sung by tavern patrons in all thirteen colonies. Published in 1768, the song captured the growing revolutionary spirit. The following is an excerpt of the lyrics:

Come join hand in hand, brave Americans all
And rouse your bold hearts at fair liberty's call
No tyrannous acts shall suppress your just claim
Or stain with dishonor America's name
Then join hand in hand brave Americans all
By uniting we stand, by dividing we fall
In so righteous a cause let us hope to succeed
For heaven approves of each generous deed
In freedom we're born and in freedom we'll live
Our purses are ready, steady friends, steady
Not as slaves, but as freemen our money we'll give.

The *Boston Chronicle* newspaper, in its August 29/September 5, 1768 edition, published the lyrics to Dickinson's song.[123] One year later, on August 14, 1769, John Adams wrote in his diary that he dined with 350 members of the Sons of Liberty at the Sign of the Liberty Tree Tavern in the Dorchester section of Boston, all of whom passionately sang the melody. Dickinson, who served as the governor of Pennsylvania and Delaware, and Joseph Reed, New Jersey's colonial secretary of state, took part in the festivities.[124]

We had two tables laid in the open field by the barn, with between 300 and
400 plates, and sail cloth overhead, and should have spent a most agreeable

day had not the rain made some abatement in our pleasures. We had also The Liberty Song…and the whole company joined in the chorus. This is cultivating the sensations of freedom.

Dickinson, along with the Pennsylvania battalion he commanded, traveled to Elizabeth in August 1776, in anticipation of a British attack on the port of New York. He earned the nickname Penman of the Revolution because of his prolific writing.[125] He wrote the first draft of the Articles of Confederation for the 1776 Continental Congress as a representative of Pennsylvania. Jane E. Calvert, PhD, the director/editor of the John Dickinson Writings Project and associate professor of history at the University of Kentucky, interviewed in July 2021, said Dickinson had many ties to New Jersey. "He had family who lived there [his brother and mother, aunts, uncles, cousins], and he vacationed there with friends. It's a safe bet that people in New Jersey taverns sang his 'New Song,' as he called it, and toasted him."

An *A* for Penmanship

The inspirational words of the Declaration of Independence came to life thanks to a son of New Jersey. Timothy Matlack, a brewer born in Haddonfield (circa 1730), is credited as having "engrossed" or handwritten (in cursive script) the Declaration of Independence onto a piece of vellum— an animal-skin parchment—that measured about thirty by twenty-four inches.[126] Matlack and his family moved to Philadelphia in the mid-1740s, where he became a brewer like his father, also named Timothy. An outspoken Patriot, Matlack served as secretary of the Continental Congress and was hailed for his meticulous penmanship on many colonial-era documents.[127]

As a Philadelphia brewer, Matlack advertised his trade in colonial newspapers.

Philadelphia brewed and bottled beer, remarkably pale and very good, to be sold by Timothy Matlack at his beer store in Fourth Street, near Market Street, for ready money only at six shillings per dozen. The cork of each bottle will be stamped "Tim Matlack Philad." No matter where throughout the Atlantic world "Masters of Vessels" happened to transport Matlack's beer, those who consumed it would always be able to identify its origins and its brewer.[128]

Portrait of Timothy Matlack painted by Charles Willson Peale, circa 1790. *Courtesy of Carolyn Cruthirds, the Museum of Fine Arts, Boston.*

The Continental Congress, on July 19, 1776, ordered Matlack to write out the Declaration of Independence.[129] *Popular Mechanics* magazine analyzed the science behind Matlack's calligraphy materials.

> *The story starts with Matlack's tools—a quill dipped in iron gall ink. It was cheap and commonly available at the time. Because of its indelibility, it was the ink of choice for documentation from the Middle Ages to the twentieth century. Its ingredients are stated in the name: ground gall nuts, taken from an oak-like tree, were boiled to draw out tannic acid, which was mixed with iron sulfate scraped from nails.*[130]

Joseph M. Vitolo writes:

> *Handwriting in the colonial period was heavily influenced by Europe, in particular England. Indeed, examining the script used by Matlack in the Declaration of Independence, one can easily see these influences. In particular, his use of English round-hand script stands out. This form of script was executed with a feather quill pen and was actually a form of* [common] *handwriting. The script is known today as Copperplate.*[131]

According to an article in the University Archives and Records Center of the University of Pennsylvania:

> *When the American Revolution came, Matlack emerged as an advocate of personal liberty and the security of property. His belief in the freedom and equality of all men led him to oppose slavery. Matlack served in military groups, one of which was the Fifth Rifle Battalion of Philadelphia Associators. As colonel of this battalion, he saw action at the Battle of Trenton in December of 1776 and then at the Battle of Princeton in January of 1777.*[132]

RALLY 'ROUND THE LIBERTY POLE

In Englewood, at the rotary intersection of West Palisade Avenue, Lafayette Avenue and Tenafly Road, a historic plaque marks the site of the town's original liberty pole and its namesake Liberty Pole Tavern.[133] Many colonies erected liberty poles, symbolizing the May 1766 repeal of the Stamp Act proposed by the British parliament as an onerous tax on a variety of paper

Liberty Pole historic marker in Englewood. *Photo by M. Gabriele.*

goods, legal documents and reading materials. A "Liberty Tree" in Boston, a gathering place for the rebellious Sons of Liberty, served as inspiration for liberty poles.[134]

Patriots in the Englewood area used the Liberty Pole Tavern to exchange ideas on the independence movement. These tavern discussions took place even while many neighbors in the village were Loyalists. "Pamphlets and broadsides from New England stimulated the cause of the Patriot colonists; chance travelers stopped for rest and refreshment at the Liberty Pole Tavern and brought the latest news gathered from the reports of various committees of correspondence throughout the colonies. Soon Bergen County decided to form a committee of correspondence."[135]

By November 1776, the mood inside the tavern had shifted drastically— from high-minded political conversations and imbibing, to serving as witness to the retreat of the Continental army.

> *On the morning of November 18, the retreat was under way. The greater part of the Continentals followed the road to Liberty Pole Tavern, thence to Old Bridge, crossing the Hackensack [River] at that point. At the fork of the road where the tavern stood, refreshment was given [to the Continental soldiers] on their weary way. The name of the [Liberty Pole Tavern] landlord has vanished from memory, but tradition relates that Washington was a guest at the tavern a few days before the retreat.*[136]

Washington used the tavern as his headquarters, where he wrote several letters. In one correspondence to Governor William Livingston, dated August 26, 1780 ("Headquarters, near the Liberty Pole, Bergen County"), he described the plight of his soldiers and their need for food.[137]

> *Some brigades of the army have been now five days without meat. To endeavor to relieve their wants by stripping the lower parts of the county of its cattle, I moved two days ago to this place....Scarcely any cattle were found, but milch [milk] cows and calves of one and two years*

old—and even those in no great plenty. When this scanty pittance is consumed, I know not to what quarter to look, as our prospects from the eastward, upon which our principal dependence is placed, are far from being favorable.

OUR DAILY BREAD

"Brewing and baking are kindred arts, just as in colonial days [when] they were twin accomplishments of every New England housewife," according to the January 1906 edition of the *Western Brewer*, a trade publication. "The similarity between brewing and baking, or beer and bread, lies in the principal material used and the process employed in both; cereals being the material, and fermentation being the process. The difference lies in the quantity of cereal and water used and the final outcome. Bread, a solid food, is baked; beer, a liquid food, is boiled. The result of fermentation in both manipulations is the same, namely the production of carbonic acid gas, sugar, and alcohol."[138]

Like beer and spirits, bread became a vital source of sustenance for the Continental army. Washington, in a July 25, 1777 letter, ordered Christopher (Christoffal) Ludwick to bake bread and have it ready for his troops at the Whitehouse Tavern in Readington (see chapter 4). "I imagine you must by this time have a considerable parcel of 'hard bread' baked. I am moving towards Philadelphia with the army, and should be glad to have it sent forward. You will continue baking as fast as you can because two other divisions will pass through Pittstown and will want bread."[139]

Tyler Putman, senior manager of gallery interpretation at the Museum of the American Revolution in Philadelphia, explained that colonial "hard bread" (called "hardtack" during the mid-1800s) was a plain biscuit made from flour, water and, occasionally, salt. Once baked, it had a long shelf life, which made it suitable as a survival ration for soldiers and seafaring travelers. Typically, it was eaten with soup or coffee. "Hard bread was essentially edible," Putman joked, referring to its tough, dry texture and bland taste. He noted that hard bread was widespread as a necessary food commodity in the colonies. Interviewed in July 2022, Putman said that, from the perspective of his museum's mission of educating the public, stories about things like soldiers eating hard bread make history more accessible for visitors. "We read about big events during the Revolutionary War, but stories about hard bread relate to everyday life."

Tyler Putman holds a bowl of fresh-baked hard bread biscuits. *Photo by Meg Bowersox, courtesy of the Museum of the American Revolution, Philadelphia.*

Two months prior to receiving the July 25 letter from Washington, Ludwick (some sources spell his name Ludwig) had been appointed "superintendent of bakers and the director of baking in the Grand Army of the United States," through a proclamation issued on May 3, 1777. Washington had petitioned Congress to find a competent individual to provide his troops with bread. The resolution stated that Ludwick had the power to license "all persons to be employed in this business and to regulate their pay, making proper report of his proceedings, and using his best endeavors to rectify all abuses in the article of bread."[140]

Following his appointment by Congress, Ludwick traveled to Morristown and oversaw the construction of high-volume, wood-fired ovens constructed from stone and iron plates and built at ground level into massive mounds of earth. Fulfilling his duties, Ludwick maintained contact with Washington and, in a January 1780 letter, provided a status report on his baking operations in Morristown:[141]

> *May it please your Excellency,*
> *Permit me to lay before you a matter of the greatest importance to an army, viz. that of supplying it with bread. With two ovens now at this place, we can furnish 1,500 loaves, of bread daily, one of said ovens is out of repair*

and ready to fall, which can be prevented by building a new one adjoining it. This will support the old one and enable me to furnish 750 loaves more per day, and amount to 2,250 loaves, which at five pounds each, would nearly supply the army.

Ludwick, born on October 17, 1720, in the town of Griessen in the province of Hesse Darmstadt in Germany, learned the baking trade from his father. He arrived in Philadelphia in 1754 and established a successful bakery business. He became an enthusiastic supporter of the Patriot movement and attended conventions in Philadelphia in the years leading up to the Declaration of Independence.[142] After establishing his ovens in Morristown, Ludwick sought out business associates in Philadelphia to help produce bread for the Continental army. One baker he enlisted was Cyrus Bustill, a mixed-race freed slave, born in Burlington on February 2, 1732. His father was a white lawyer named Samuel Bustill. Samuel died when Cyrus was ten years old, and the family sold Cyrus to a friend, a baker and influential Quaker named Thomas Pryor. Cyrus learned the craft and earned his freedom in 1769.[143] He started a baking business in Burlington and then moved to Philadelphia, where he prospered as a baker and a brewer. Aligned with Ludwick, Bustill baked bread for Washington's troops.

Following the Revolutionary War, Bustill became an abolitionist, a prominent member of Philadelphia's African American community and an early supporter of the Free African Society. (The group created its preamble articles on April 12, 1787, and finalized the articles on May 17, 1787.) Later that same year, on September 18, Bustill addressed a forum in Philadelphia. Most likely, this event was organized as part of Bustill's outreach as a member of the Free African Society. He spoke out on freedom, equality, religious charity and mercy and his journey through slavery. Bustill also addressed the evils of alcohol abuse ("rum drinking"), which he said plagued the African American community.[144]

Let me caution you, my brethren, against that crying sin of drunkenness that is so much in fashion; that abominable practice of rum drinking to excess and so hurtful to men of our color; yea, and women, too, are fond of it. My fellow men, I would wish us to remember no drunkard can enter the kingdom [of heaven]. I believe I have seen more [men] who have shortened their days by this dreadful practice. I am not a young man; I am in the fifty-sixth year of my age, and have had time to reflect on things past. I have seen numbers laid in graves.

Ludwick died in Philadelphia on June 17, 1801. Five years later, Bustill also died in Philadelphia. He's the great-great-grandfather of Paul Robeson, the renowned New Jersey actor, singer, scholar, activist and 1919 Rutgers College valedictorian.

CHAPTER 3

"THE TIMES THAT TRY MEN'S SOULS"

"A MONUMENT IN THE HEARTS OF ALL LOVERS OF LIBERTY"

Bravery, tragedy, sacrifice, victory and defeat—these were the human experiences during the Revolutionary War years. Days passed when the outcome of the conflict was, at best, uncertain. Ill-equipped, bedraggled Patriot soldiers struggled to stay alive, enduring the toll of bitter winters and broiling summers, with little to eat and forced to make do with ragged clothing and worn-out boots. Village taverns offered solace and served as makeshift military headquarters.

Thomas Paine, Founding Father, political philosopher and influential author during the Revolutionary War—who published landmark books and pamphlets (*The American Crisis*, *Common Sense*, *The Age of Reason*, *Rights of Man*)—had a special place in his heart for the village of Bordentown. In a letter to a friend, written in 1789, Paine quipped: "I rather see my horse, Button, in his own stable, or eating the grass of Bordentown…than see all the pomp and show of Europe."[145]

Paine's favorite watering hole in Bordentown, where he lived between 1778 and 1787, was the Washington House, a tavern kept by Deborah Applegate and owned by John J. Rodgers. "This place was Mr. Paine's principal resort, and here he had many contests with gentlemen whom he met. It must be remembered in the olden days [that] taverns were not dignified with the name of hotels, and were not frequented by promiscuous customers, but

The Washington House *(far right building)*, Bordentown. *Photo courtesy of Doug Kiovsky, Bordentown Historical Society.*

were the resort of gentlemen of means, principally. Furnished with ample arm chairs and tables, they possessed some of the comforts of club rooms, and the conversations or arguments were conducted with great decorum."[146] While Paine socialized at the Washington House, "only brandy and atheism passed his lips. As a matter of fact, Paine was a deist, not an atheist."[147]

Doug Kiovsky of the Bordentown Historical Society, interviewed in August 2021, said one reason Paine frequented the Washington House was because "it had stables located in the back that accommodated his horse, Button." Located at the corner of Farnsworth Avenue and Crosswicks Street, the Washington House was razed around 1933. Kiovsky said Hoagland's Tavern, owned by Major Oakley Hoagland and located at the intersection of Farnsworth Avenue and Park Street, became another popular spot in Bordentown. It originally was known as the Black Horse Tavern, until Hoagland acquired it in 1774. A local militia officer, Hoagland's duties involved disrupting smuggling along the waterways by the British. His tavern became the site of joyful celebrations in 1783, following the signing of the Treaty of Paris. Kiovsky said a fire destroyed much of Hoagland's tavern and it was subsequently demolished on September 17, 1984.

Paine bought a home in Bordentown. Gary Berton, president of the Thomas Paine National Historical Association, headquartered in New Rochelle, New York, said Paine's Bordentown house, which he sold in

Hoagland's Tavern. *Photo courtesy of Doug Kiovsky, Bordentown Historical Society.*

1808, was on the corner of Farnsworth Avenue and Church Street. The house still stands. "Paine owned the house, but never lived in it," Berton explained during an interview in September 2021. "He stayed with his friend [Revolutionary War officer] Colonel Joseph Kirkbride. The Kirkbride house was large and Paine was said to occupy a second-floor bedroom." Berton said Paine became a familiar figure in Bordentown, taking daily strolls "with his hat held behind his back."

A statue of Paine can be found in the Hilltop section of Bordentown, adjacent to the site of where Kirkbride's home, 2 Farnsworth Avenue, known as New Bellevue, once stood. Kiovsky explained that Kirkbride located his estate near a ferry slip at the mouth of the Crosswicks Creek, which gave him ready access to the Delaware River.

Paine enlisted in the Continental army in August 1776. One month later, he was stationed in Fort Lee, where he served as an aide-de-camp to General Nathanael Greene. Paine marched through New Jersey with the troops during the 1776 retreat. His celebrated pamphlet *The American Crisis* included the iconic line, "These are the times that try men's souls."[148] Writing like a war correspondent, Paine documented the first critical point in the retreat, a site in today's River Edge, Bergen County, known as the New Bridge Landing, which is designated with a historic plaque. After reaching Newark, he began recording his thoughts, "an appeal to the people in this hour of crisis."

> *I have as little superstition in me as any man living, but my secret opinion has ever been, and still is, that God Almighty will not give up a people to military destruction, or leave them unsupportedly to perish, who have so earnestly and so repeatedly sought to avoid the calamities of war, by every decent method which wisdom could invent....We* [stayed] *four days at Newark, collected our outposts with some of the Jersey militia, and marched out twice to meet the enemy, on being informed that they were advancing, though our numbers were greatly inferior to theirs....Would that heaven might inspire some Jersey maid to spirit up her countrymen, and save her fair fellow sufferers from ravage and ravishment!*

Berton said Paine's vision of a heavenly "Jersey maid" is a poetic reference to a transcendent, spiritual figure like Joan of Arc (the fifteenth-century national heroine of France), to be a symbol of the Revolution and the cause of independence, no matter the odds. He went to Philadelphia and published the narrative in the December 19, 1776 edition of the *Pennsylvania Journal*.

During his years in England before coming to America, Paine worked as an activist, opposed to the political dominance of the monarchy, the hereditary aristocracy and religious rulers. Appointed as an excise officer (a tax assessor) on February 19, 1768, Paine frequented the White Hart Inn, a tavern in Lewes, a village in East Sussex.[149] Paine and the local intelligentsia met at the White Hart to drink, debate and critique each other's philosophical concepts. They referred to themselves as the Headstrong Club. Berton said members of this circle at the White Hart recognized Paine as a local celebrity—a skilled author, orator and critical thinker. The White Hart's regulars had what they called the Headstrong Book. "[It was given] to the most obstinate haranguer in the club," implying that Paine frequently earned that distinction.

Paine traveled between Lewes and London during the years 1772 and 1774 to meet with Benjamin Franklin and attend lectures on science and politics, according to Berton. Franklin went to London in 1757 to serve as a diplomat and a representative of the Pennsylvania Assembly. He returned to Philadelphia in 1775 to support the Revolution.[150] Documents and letters written by Paine, compiled by the Thomas Paine National Historical Association, indicate the two men first met around 1760, became friends and remained in touch. Berton said George Lewis Scott, a famed British mathematician, literary figure and commissioner of excise, introduced Paine to Franklin. A guess—and only a guess—on the part of this author is that the meetings between Franklin and Paine might have occurred at

Statue of Thomas Paine in Bordentown. *Photo by M. Gabriele.*

Franklin's favorite London haunts. Franklin frequented Paul's Head Tavern on Cateaton Street[151] (today known as Gresham Street, not far from Saint Paul's Cathedral) and the Smyrna Coffee House, located on the north side of Pall Mall, a boulevard adjacent to Saint James Square.[152] "Franklin was no stranger to the popular politics of London. He frequented the coffee houses of London and joined the Club of Honest Whigs."[153]

Franklin recognized Paine's abilities and believed he would be successful in America. Franklin provided a letter of recommendation to Paine, dated September 30, 1774. Paine left England in October and arrived in Philadelphia on November 30, 1774. Soon after landing, Paine began working at *Pennsylvania Magazine*. On January 10, 1776, he published the widely distributed booklet *Common Sense*, with the subtitle "Addressed to the Inhabitants of America," which helped spark the cause of independence.[154]

"By the 1790s, Thomas Paine was the most famous person in the world," Berton declared. "He's the father of the modern, global democratic movement. It all starts with Paine." Berton said Paine put into words progressive principles such as "all men are created equal" and "the separation of church and state," which are among the foundations of American democracy. He aligned himself with England's Whig Patriot politics, which promoted a representative parliamentary system of individual rights and defended political dissent.

Andrew Jackson (nicknamed Old Hickory), the seventh president of the United States, who joined a Continental army militia in South Carolina in 1779 at the age of thirteen, became a loyal admirer of Paine. Jackson once had a conversation with Judge Thomas Hertell, a progressive lawyer and philanthropist from New York. The discussion involved Hertell's desire to explore ways to commemorate Paine's achievements during the Revolutionary War. President Jackson assured Hertell that wouldn't be necessary. "Thomas Paine needs no monument made by hands," Jackson said. "He has erected a monument in the hearts of all lovers of liberty."[155]

THE BRAVE FERRYMEN

The Johnson Ferry House and Tavern, a tourist attraction at Washington Crossing State Park in Titusville, Mercer County, sits peacefully in a field, not far from the Delaware River. But in the frigid, early morning hours of Christmas Day, 1776, the inhabitants of the house—James Slack, the brave ferryman, and his family—played a significant role in assisting George

Washington and the Continental army in their crossing of the Delaware, which led to the victory over the Hessians in Trenton—a critical turning point in the Revolutionary War.

The Johnson house is the lone structure still standing associated with Washington's historic river crossing. Rutger Jansen (his Dutch last name anglicized to Johnson) and his son Garret built the ferry house in 1740 and ran what must have been a lucrative business, shuttling farmers and merchants across the Delaware River. Eventually, Garret needed to obtain a license to run the ferry and did so in 1761. Slack (the anglicized version of his Dutch last name, Sleght), a Presbyterian Patriot citizen and a strong supporter of the Continental army's cause, started operating the Delaware River ferry in 1767, one year after Garret Johnson died, according to park historian Nancy Ceperley Deal, interviewed in August 2021. Along with a ferry license, Slack also applied for and received a tavern license to boost his profits by providing lodging, drink and food for his ferry passengers.

Ceperley Deal said Slack's ferry house operated as a "guest" tavern—a more modest business compared with a fully stocked village tavern. Tavern guests would eat whatever was being served for the family's supper, drink whatever alcoholic beverages Slack had on hand and then find a spot on the floor to spend the night.

Johnson Ferry House and Tavern, Washington Crossing State Park, Titusville. *Photo by M. Gabriele.*

Statue of George Washington on horseback, Morristown. *Photo by M. Gabriele.*

Pursued by the British army, the Continental army's historic retreat came to a halt when it arrived at the banks of the Delaware River in Trenton on December 2, 1776.[156] "Washington had sent orders ahead for boats, and many were waiting when they arrived. For the next five days the men labored mightily at getting their guns, supplies and wagons across the river."[157] Washington made his headquarters at the Keith House in Upper Makefield Township, Pennsylvania, and with his officers, hatched plans for their attack on Trenton.

One dramatic element in this story involves Continental army soldiers, prior to crossing the Delaware River back to New Jersey, becoming motivated by the inspirational words contained in Thomas Paine's *American Crisis* pamphlet. "There is no concrete evidence, but there is a lot of circumstantial evidence that supports the fact that the troops, before crossing the Delaware, had [Paine's words] read aloud to them," Gary Berton said. "Multiple copies were printed in pamphlet form, which were quickly sent out of Philadelphia, and Paine would have had them go first to Washington. The pamphlets arrived on December 22, 1776, indicating it got priority. It may have been a mixture of officers reading it aloud to their detachments, or just circulating the document informally. It makes more sense that if one officer did it, others would follow. No historian has ever questioned that it was used to rally the troops in some manner."

A winter storm hit the region on Christmas 1776, just as the Continental army began mobilizing to cross the river back to New Jersey, which made the transit even more risky. In addition to seeking help from Delaware River ferrymen like Slack, the Continental army had experienced watermen within its ranks. Colonel John Glover's Marblehead regiment "was filled with New Englanders who had extensive experience as seamen. Glover's men were all quite identifiable with their short blue seaman's jackets, tarred pants, and woolen caps. Other experienced watermen from the Philadelphia area, many familiar with this exact stretch of river, had also congregated in the area and were able to provide the muscle and skill needed to make the perilous nighttime crossing."[158] Ceperley Deal concurred, adding that the "Marbleheaders" were cod fishermen who knew how to handle boats in a storm. "They weren't going to be intimidated by crossing a river." In addition to the Marbleheaders, historian David Hackett Fischer said mariners from the Philadelphia waterfront came to the aid of the army: seamen, longshoremen, block makers, riggers and ships' carpenters, along with "ferrymen and boatmen from New Jersey and Pennsylvania, who knew the river and could navigate it in the dark."[159]

William M. Welsch, in an essay, explains there was another ferry line on the Pennsylvania side of the Delaware, known as McKonkey's Ferry, operated by Samuel McKonkey, who also kept a tavern.[160]

Two ferries and their adjacent houses or taverns served the traveling population at this site—McKonkey's on the Pennsylvania side and Johnson's Ferry [operated by James Slack] on the Jersey side. As ferries were licensed by the individual states, it was not unusual to have two such ferries in such close proximity with different names. But essentially, this was one ferry crossing. There were no docks, but rather roads that sloped down to the landing to accommodate teams and wagons as they rolled on or off the ferry boats.

The ferry or flat boats themselves, which were to play a crucial role in the crossing, were large enough to accommodate the freight wagons and teams as well as the smaller farm vehicles that would constitute their regular customers. The boats were flat-bottomed scows with low sides and hinged front and rear ramps. Ferrymen propelled them across the river using cables fixed to the shore and a system of pulleys, ropes and setting poles.

Welsch, an author, historian and the founding member and president of the American Revolution Round Table of Richmond, Virginia, served for over three decades as an administrator at Montclair State University.

Reenactment of Washington crossing the Delaware River. *Photo courtesy of Wayne Henderek, resource interpretive specialist, Washington Crossing State Park.*

Ceperley Deal said Slack, his son Richard, grandson Uriah and nephew James Henry Slack answered the urgent call to duty and, as experienced ferrymen, helped navigate the army, artillery and horses across the river. Two types of vessels were employed in the river crossing. Durham boats, designed like large canoes with high walls, were rowed across the Delaware, carrying soldiers. River craft for the crossing also included scows, as noted by Welsch. The scows were strong enough to transport the Continental army's horses and artillery.

According to Ceperley Deal, as the storm intensified and the soldiers reassembled on the New Jersey side of the river, tradition has it that Washington and his generals huddled inside Slack's tavern. She said this was "an informed guess," considering the harsh weather conditions, the need to find suitable shelter in order to review strategies and the practice of Revolutionary War army officers temporarily commandeering homes when needed. The Continental army "trekked inland to the Bear Tavern and turned right [at or near today's County Route 579 in Hopewell Township], heading southeast toward Trenton. They crossed Jacob's Creek and entered present-day Ewing Township." The Continental army attacked the Hessians in Trenton—a victory for the Americans.[161]

Historic plaque from the Daughters of the American Revolution marking Washington's crossing of the Delaware River. *Photo by M. Gabriele.*

The river crossing on December 25, 1776, is part of the "ten crucial days," the campaign that turned the Revolutionary War in favor of the Patriots. Jennifer Dowling Norato, this book's peer editor, said a young Alexander Hamilton made a name for himself during the river crossing. In March 1776, Hamilton received the appointment as captain of the Provincial Company of Artillery for New York, after declining two aide-de-camp requests. Hamilton's leadership and quick thinking were critical, Norato said. "As they neared the north of Trenton, the wooden wheels of the artillery pieces and lumbering ammunition carts...were very likely wrapped in old blankets and cloth to muffle the creaking noise" in order to maintain the element of surprise.[162]

Ceperley Deal, who has worked as a historian at the state park since 1986, said people should take pride in this story because civilians like tavern owner James Slack "were front-line heroes. They helped the army cross the Delaware River and saved many lives. The role of ferrymen, farmers and tavern keepers [was] critical to the success of the Continental Army's cause."

NEWARK'S FAVORITE GENERAL

Prior to the historic Delaware River crossing, after crossing the Passaic River on November 21, 1776, during the famous retreat, Washington ordered his troops to burn the bridge in order to thwart the pursuit of the British army. A plaque in Passaic marks the spot of the crossing at the Acquackanonk Bridge. The retreat began with the British army overwhelming Patriot forces at Fort Washington along the Hudson River in New York on November 16. Washington had his sights set on regrouping in Newark and

Historic plaque in Passaic marking Washington's crossing at the Acquackanonk Bridge. *Photo by M. Gabriele.*

finding a suitable temporary headquarters at a Newark tavern. It's presumed that Washington led the march to Newark along the west side of the Passaic River, along a path that followed today's River Road.[163]

Once settled in Newark, Washington wrote a letter to John Hancock, dated November 23, 1776:[164]

> *The situation of our affairs is truly critical and…requires uncommon exertions on our part. From the movements of the enemy and the information we have received, they certainly will make a push to possess themselves of this part of the Jersey.*

Washington didn't identify the name or location of his Newark headquarters in the letter, which has led to conjecture among historians. Perhaps he changed headquarters several times during his brief stay in Newark in order to evade British spies. Author Joseph Atkinson wrote that Washington arrived in Newark on the evening of November 22, 1776.

> *Here* [in Newark] *Washington and the Patriot army remained, from the evening of the twenty-second until the morning of the twenty-eighth* [of November]. *It is very unlikely that Washington, who was nothing if not cautious in the matter of providing against military surprises, would establish his headquarters in the upper portion of town, comparatively close to where the pursuing enemy might appear at any moment. The burden of probability, if not of proof, points to the old Eagle Tavern as the Washington headquarters in Newark. This hostelry occupied a site fronting on Broad Street* [near the intersection of William Street], *and stood back on ground a little north of where the City Hall now stands. It was a large, rough stone, two-story house, with wooden outbuildings. On its sign was perched, with the recollection of old people, the national bird of freedom.*[165]

Atkinson's research for his book would have occurred one hundred years after Washington's 1776 stay in Newark, so it's plausible that the "recollection of old people" was the memories and oral history handed down to citizens just two generations after the general's stay in Newark. Atkinson wrote that "within the memory of many persons still living, [the Eagle Tavern] was known and spoken of generally as the 'Washington Headquarters.' After undergoing various changes and serving at one time as a temporary court house, [the tavern] was torn down to give place to the City Hotel—the present City Hall."

Another author, Frank John Urquhart, identifies Josiah Pierson as the tavern keeper at the Eagle.

> *We learn of a hostelry at what is now the north corner of Broad and William streets, the Eagle Tavern…an inn kept by Captain* [Josiah] *Pierson during the War. It may have been either the Rising Sun or the Eagle. The Rising Sun seems to have been continued after the war began. Travelers going to New York passed up or down Broad Street to Market and then eastward to the ferry across the Passaic* [River], *over the meadows to the Hackensack* [River] *and on over Bergen Hill to the inn at Paulus Hook* [Jersey City], *whence they took a ferry to New York. It seems to have been a famous place of entertainment in its time but, unfortunately, the records of its day are exasperatingly meager.*[166]

Washington also visited Newark in 1775. The second Continental Congress, meeting in Philadelphia, unanimously selected him as the commander in chief of the Continental army on June 15, 1775.[167] He and his military advisers left Philadelphia on June 23 bound for Cambridge, Massachusetts, where he was to take command of the army there (he arrived in Cambridge on July 2). Newark historian Charles F. Cummings wrote about Washington's visit in one of his columns, "Knowing Newark." "Washington's first trip to Newark took place on June 24, 1775, when the commander in chief stopped off on his way to Cambridge. The general is thought to have stayed at the Eagle Tavern."[168] Washington's familiarity with this tavern on this visit is an indication that he likely chose the same establishment for his headquarters one year later during the historic retreat.

Cummings writes that when Washington returned to Newark during the 1776 retreat, "the mood of this trip was entirely different. No longer excited over the possibility of victory, [Washington's] fortunes seemed exhausted. His army was in rags, his men hungry. Newarkers were noted for their hospitality, and on more than one occasion Washington was treated to ham and eggs. The hostess hoped that seconds were not requested, because in most cases there were none."

Washington returned to Newark during the winter of 1779–80 while he was touring encampments at Morristown and dined at the home of Captain Nathaniel Camp, which was located at Broad and Camp Streets, according to Cummings. He wrote that Newark expressed its fondness and respect for the general when he passed away on December 14, 1799, at his estate in Mount Vernon, Virginia. "Washington's death in 1799 brought the final

Statue depicting George Washington at Harriet Tubman Square, Newark. John Massey Rhind created the statue, which was unveiled on November 2, 1912. *Photo by M. Gabriele.*

chapter in the relationship between the city and the general. Notice of his death was met at the Essex County Courthouse by a resolution for residents to wear black crepe arm bands, the tolling of bells, and funeral orations by churches and Masonic lodges. The following year, February 22, was proclaimed a citywide day of mourning [and] so ended Newark's first-hand relationship with a national hero, the father of the country."

A Civil War

The bitter partisan divide between Patriots and Loyalists created serious rifts among family members, friends and business associates—people who once drank together and socialized in taverns. Community members were enlisted to gather information, locate the storage of supplies or spy on the movements of the competing armies. Occasionally, there were violent confrontations. Author Rick Schwertfeger said financial, religious and political issues were part of the Patriot/Loyalist conflict. Based in Texas, Schwertfeger grew up in Bergen County. "Some Loyalists agreed with the rebels, but the Loyalists favored negotiations with England, not a revolt," he said in a January 2021 interview. "They considered themselves to be loyal British subjects. They were people who had succeeded in the New Jersey colony in business and politics and were trying to maintain their self-interests."

Schwertfeger writes,

My northern New Jersey hometown of Bergenfield—then called Schraalenburgh—became a center of the Loyalist/Patriot "civil war" during the American Revolution. Its Dutch Huguenot settlers followed the Dutch Reformed religion; and had memories of themselves or their elders fleeing Europe from religious oppression. As changing European alliances impacted the American colonies during the seventeenth century, these passionate colonials were strongly anti-Tory. The reasons for Loyalist allegiance to Britain ran the gamut. Whatever their dissatisfactions with how the colonies were treated, rebellion was unconscionable. Some had experienced commercial, financial, and/or political success in America, and aimed to protect their wealth and positions. Interestingly, some quite agreed with the dissatisfactions of the rebels. As revolutionary fervor increased, the position of many Loyalists became quite untenable. The circumstances that created Loyalists often were less about ideology and more about material issues. Labeled Tories by the Patriots, they became the enemy. Many prominent Loyalists fled the colonies for safety. Some returned to England. A large number fled to Canada.[169]

"Loyalists and Patriots absolutely shared political ideas," declared Dr. Christopher F. Minty, a scholar who serves as the managing editor of the John Dickinson Writings Project at the Center for Digital Editing at the University of Virginia. Minty, interviewed in March 2021, added that, like the Loyalists, Patriots also had business and political interests to consider. Minty questioned whether the American Revolution could even be considered a civil war. "Or, is framing the Revolution as a civil war another way to package the conflict with hopes of making it more appealing? However packaged, framing the American Revolution as a civil war is hard. It does not fit neatly alongside other civil wars."

Minty writes,

Conceptualizing the American Revolution as a civil war, moreover, suggests that there were coherent groups of Loyalists and Patriots—groups which were in consistent opposition to one another. It didn't work out that way, though. People changed sides as their wartime circumstances changed.

The Revolution wasn't a simple conflict between Loyalists and Patriots. People didn't always have the luxury to "choose their own loyalty"; under strenuous circumstances, they were forced to make a decision. Put simply, their loyalty was often enforced. The problem of allegiance thus begs the question: Can we really use the term "civil war" to describe a conflict involving [markedly different] *people, who were not opposed to changing sides? Indeed, we must remember at all times that my American Revolution wasn't necessarily yours.*[170]

The drama between Loyalists and Patriots, neighbor against neighbor, played out in Hunterdon County involving the Vought House, built in 1759 by the Vought family, and Captain Thomas Jones's Tavern. Jones, a member of the Patriots' Hunterdon County militia, established Jones Tavern, about a mile away from the Vought house. Donald E. Sherblom, PhD, an author, historian and member of the 1759 Vought House organization, outlines a clash that took place on June 24, 1776. Jones was a Patriot, while members of the

Vought House historic marker. *Photo by M. Gabriele.*

well-to-do Vought family were supporters of British rule of the colonies. Sherblom wrote that the Voughts' 488-acre homestead was a successful farm, producing hay, wheat and Indian corn while raising sheep, cattle and hogs. The homestead had a business partnership with the nearby Union Iron Works facility. "The many iron workers, charcoal colliers [producers], and miners [at the Union Iron Works] provided a natural market for the Vought farmstead's produce."[171]

Members of the Vought family issued and signed the license for Captain Jones's tavern. A proclamation dated May 3, 1775, stated that "whereas Thomas Jones of Lebanon Township, having kept a public house of entertainment for these several years past, and always kept good order in this house; and we the neighbors [believe] there is a necessity for a tavern to be continued there; your petitioners humbly beg your honorable worship will be pleased to grant the said Thomas Jones a license to continue a tavern where he now dwelleth."[172]

Interviewed in February 2021, Sherblom said tensions came to a head in 1775 and 1776, and the friendship between the Vought family and

Vought House, Clinton. *Photo by M. Gabriele.*

Jones deteriorated. The Provincial Congress called on John Vought, son of Christoffel Vought, to "turn out" volunteers (Union Iron Works employees) for the local Patriot militia, but he refused. As a result, they were ordered to appear before the congress on June 24, 1776. This move triggered an angry response that night. A mob of two dozen men, mostly workers from the Union Iron Works, led by John Vought, stormed Jones's Tavern. They roughed up Captain Jones, damaged his property and threatened his family. Jones filed a deposition to protest the raid. Two days later, the Provisional Congress and the Council of Safety of New Jersey directed Colonel Abraham Ten Eyck and his militia to apprehend John Vought, his associates and members of the Union Iron Works mob.[173]

Christoffel and John Vought, along with John Allen, the manager of the ironworks, were captured and imprisoned in Trenton for two weeks. After their release, the Voughts continued to support the British army and organized a Loyalist militia. "The Vought family had little to gain from a political upheaval," Sherblom writes, but events and sentiment in Hunterdon County turned against the Voughts. In the spring of 1779, the Patriot government confiscated the Voughts' stone house and farm. Ironically, the house and property were sold at auction at Thomas Jones's tavern. Following the 1783 Treaty of Paris, the Vought family sailed to Nova Scotia, according to Sherblom, just as many other Loyalists did following the end of the war.

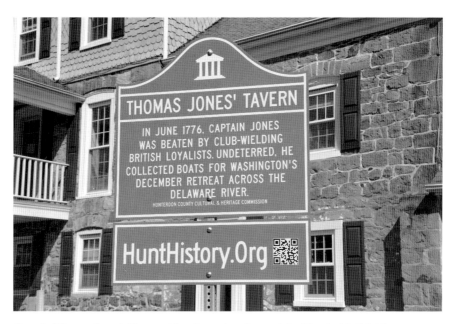

Captain Thomas Jones's Tavern, historic marker, Annandale. *Photo by M. Gabriele.*

Captain Thomas Jones's Tavern, Annandale. *Photo by M. Gabriele.*

Interviewed in March 2021, West Orange historian extraordinaire Joe Fagan told the story about the Williams family and Tory Corner during the 1770s.[174]

[Nathaniel and Mary Williams] *were married in 1775 and lived in a small farm house near the current intersection of Eagle Rock and Harrison Avenues. They were considered well-to-do planters with rich holdings. Nathaniel's younger brother Benjamin lived in the same area and enjoyed an equally prosperous existence. Both were ingrained with a deep loyalty to the British Crown and remained outspoken about their profound allegiance with England. They frequently met with other Loyalists near the present day intersection of Washington and Main Streets* [known at the time as Swinefield Road and Valley Road]. *This area originally was called Williamsville, but it soon took on the name of Tory Corner, by which it is still known today.*

Fagan said Swinefield Road, so named because it was a route used by drovers guiding their pigs and cattle from the pastures of the West Orange region to the markets of Newark, became a major thoroughfare during this period as a passage through the Watchung Mountains.

Tory Corner monument, West Orange. *Photo by M. Gabriele.*

Today, a monument marks the site of Tory Corner, which became a platform for people espousing Loyalist political views, with Nathaniel Williams a leading voice among his neighbors. Williams and his cronies would have had other establishments for drinking and discussing politics. The first tavern in the Orange area was located at the corner of Main and Hillyer Streets. During this period, the hamlet was known as Orange Dale. The hostelry opened around the year 1755. "A tavern or place of entertainment of man and beast was one of the necessary evils of the time." A tavern keeper named Samuel Munn was the first dispenser of provender (food or animal fodder) and Jersey Lightning.[175]

RUNAWAY

As described in chapter 2 ("Read All About It"), taverns were places of reading, inviting haunts to discuss politics, business and topics of daily colonial life. Stagecoaches delivered colonial newspapers, and tavern customers caught up on current events, sometimes reading articles aloud for the benefit of others. But information printed on pages of eighteenth-century newspapers also documented another story: the cruel business of slavery that existed in New Jersey and other colonies. Just like news about the sale of taverns, newspapers posted advertisements about runaway enslaved people and indentured servants and offers of rewards for their capture, along with warnings not to assist or shelter them. Transcribed newspaper advertisements gave detailed descriptions of runaways:

> *Run away from the subscriber living at Bergen in New Jersey on Wednesday the 30th of July, a Negro fellow named Robin, about twenty-five years of age, five feet, eight inches high and speaks good Dutch and English, this country born, is a slim fellow and had a down look. Had on, when he went away, a blue cloth jacket and tow* [baggy] *trousers. Whoever takes up and secures the said fellow, if in New York, shall have forty shillings, and if out of the province of New York, three pounds. And all reasonable charges paid by Thomas Brown in New York or George Codiments. All masters of vessels and others are forbid to carry him off or harbor him.*
> —The New York Mercury, *August 4, 1760*[176]

> *Five dollars reward; run away from "Boontown"* [Boonton], *in the county of Morris and the province of New Jersey, on Sunday the eighteenth of October last: a negro man named Mingo or Tim. He is about thirty years of age, has a scar either on his nose or one of his cheeks, is about five feet seven or eight inches high, plays on the violin, speaks good Dutch and English and is much addicted to strong drink. Had on when he went away a dark brown broad coat with brass Philadelphia buttons, a brown broad cloth waist coat with basket mohair buttons, a pair of red coating trousers, and wool hat. Whoever apprehends said negro and returns him to his master, or secures him in any of his majesty's gaols, shall be paid the above reward and all reasonable charges.*
> —The New York Gazette and the Weekly Mercury, *November 30, 1772*[177]

First Rhode Island regiment reenactors portray members of Lord Dunsmore's Loyal Ethiopian Regiment, a Loyalist unit of freed slaves commanded by Virginia's royal governor. *Photo by M. Gabriele.*

On April 14, 1775, a group of men met at the Rising Sun Tavern in Pennsylvania, located at the intersection of Germantown and York Roads, about four miles north of Philadelphia, to establish the first abolition society in the United States. They "adopted a constitution to establish a group they called The Society for the Relief of Free Negroes, Unlawfully Held in Bondage." Revolutionary War activities disrupted the group, but it reorganized nine years later. "In 1787 a new constitution was adopted, the name was changed, and Benjamin Franklin was elected president. Two years later the [Pennsylvania] state legislature granted it a charter of incorporation. Most of its supporters were the Friends [Quakers] who had been so active against slavery in the earlier days."[178]

The Diary of Robert Morton cross-references the existence of the Rising Sun Tavern. Morton (1760–1786), a Quaker, penned a journal as a teenager while the British army occupied Philadelphia. In a December 8, 1777 entry in his diary, he wrote, "The Hessians on their march committed great outrages on the inhabitants....Set fire to the house on Germantown Road, called the Rising Sun, and committed many other depredations, as if the sole purpose of the expedition was to destroy and to spread desolation and ruin."[179]

For a comprehensive examination of the history of slavery in the Garden State, this author recommends the book Stories of Slavery in New Jersey *by Rick Geffken, published by The History Press.*

"A Gentle Man Who Spoke Persuasively"

John Woolman became a leading figure in New Jersey's abolitionist movement. Woolman, a Quaker born in the backwoods region of Rancocas (today's Mount Holly), gained recognition as a talented orator at the June 27, 1743 quarterly meeting of Quaker ministers and elders, held in Burlington. Following this meeting, Woolman and an elderly Quaker preacher named Abraham Farrington went on a tour of New Jersey, preaching a message of faith and tolerance. They set out on September 5, 1743, and spoke one evening at a tavern in New Brunswick, "in which none of our [Quaker] society dwelt. They had a large and attentive congregation. The room was full and the people quiet."[180]

Charles Bruder, the executive director of the John Woolman Memorial Association in Mount Holly, said Woolman often sought out taverns to address village residents. "Taverns were a convenient landing place to meet local people. Woolman's gatherings would have been spontaneous happenings, open to the entire community: Quakers and non-Quakers, men, women and children." Bruder, interviewed in July 2022, explained that it was a common practice for traveling preachers to use taverns as venues to connect with an eighteenth-century audience. Word would have spread quickly about such an event, and it was also good business for a tavern to attract a crowd. "Woolman did condemn drunkenness, but he wasn't against the tavern business, which provided food and lodging in addition to alcohol."

During the 1760s, Woolman was well aware of tavern culture in Mount Holly.

Daniel Jones, who kept the Three Tuns Tavern, was the elder brother of Woolman's friend, Rebecca Jones. The old tavern yards were busy places when the stage came in, and there [was] a delightful bit of local color in the visit of the juggler to the tavern. He [the juggler] had been well advertised and was so successful that his show was to be repeated the next night. One sees John Woolman sitting at the [tavern] entrance and, when the people had gathered, can almost hear his clear and quiet remonstrance and his sweet invitation to think on higher things.[181]

During his travels, Woolman voiced his opposition to slavery. "Woolman was a gentle man who spoke persuasively to slave owners about the evils of slave ownership and was often able to convince them, without causing offence, to release their slaves."[182] Woolman "belonged to a group of Quakers in New Jersey and Pennsylvania who organized the first effective campaign to turn the Society of Friends officially against slavery. He traveled from North Carolina to Massachusetts visiting Quaker meetings, holding private conferences with slaveholding Friends, writing further essays and petitioning Quaker meetings. In none of these activities was he alone."[183]

TAVERN PATRONS ALSO READ about the struggles of European indentured servants. "The demand for labor in the American colonies…led to various schemes to promote immigration and especially to enable the laboring class to overcome great obstacles, presented by a long and expensive journey. In England and on the continent [Europe] there was an abundant supply of laborers, but the majority of those disposed to seek homes and employment in the colonies were too poor to transport themselves."[184] Indentured servants "were those immigrants who, unable to pay their passage, signed a contract called an 'indenture' before embarking, in which they agreed with the master or owner of the vessel transporting them 'to serve him or his assigns' a period of years in return for passage to America." In New Jersey and the other colonies, there was a vast demand for servant labor to operate and maintain homes, farms and businesses. Young European men and women, aware of potential opportunities in the New World, apparently were willing to gamble their futures for the promise of a better life. Based on the advertisements appearing in the colonial newspapers, some indentured servants, after enduring harsh treatment, tried to escape from their masters.

Run away on the thirteenth of last month from the subscriber living in Bordentown. A likely servant lad named Patrick Weldon is a native of Ireland and has something of the brogue on his tongue, about nineteen years of age and a fair complexion. Had on and took with him a felt hat, an old brown vest…leather breeches that has been dyed black but are much faded, with metal buttons, yarn stockings, old shoes. Whoever will secure him, so that his master may have him again, shall have three pounds reward and reasonable charges paid by me, Edward Pancoast. It

is supposed he will get to sea. He pretends to be something of a sailor, therefore this serves to forewarn all masters of vessels not to carry him off, at their own peril.
—The New York Mercury, *March 1, 1756*

Run away on the twentieth of October last in Amwell, in the county of Hunterdon Province of New Jersey, a High Dutch servant woman named Anna Catherina Michtilin. Has a down look, of middle stature, well set, about twenty-five or twenty-six years of age, much freckled, has black eyes and black hair. Had with her a female child about a year old with dark eyes. Had on her when she went away a blue and white striped Linsey [cheap and durable] *woolsey gown, a black and white striped Linsey petticoat, a pair of moss-colored stocking, new footed, and old shoes.*
—The Pennsylvania Journal, *November 3, 1757*[185]

Taverns came under legal scrutiny for their suspected business dealings with Indigenous and enslaved people and indentured servants. A session of the New Jersey General Assembly, which met in Burlington from December 7, 1713, to March 17, 1714, passed legislation on March 11 titled "An Act for Regulating of Slaves": "Be it enacted by the governor, council and general assembly and by the authority of the same, that all and every person or persons within this province, who shall at any time after publication hereof, buy, sell, barter, trade or traffic with any Negro, Indian or mulatto slave, for any rum, wine, beer, cider or other strong drink…shall pay for the first offense twenty shillings and for the second and every other offense forty shillings." Thirty-seven years later, the New Jersey General Assembly enacted another bill titled "An Act to Restrain Tavern Keepers and Others from Selling Spirituous Liquors to Servants, Negroes and Mulatto Slaves." The legislation passed on October 25, 1751, and called on tavern owners to take an oath swearing that they would not sell strong liquor to enslaved people without the master's consent.[186]

Author Graham Russell Hodges writes that such restrictions during these years were difficult to enforce. "Despite the laws against selling liquor to slaves, tavern keepers and grocers found the profits irresistible. In the countryside, blacks purchased rum without much difficulty. Account books from rural New Jersey record free blacks and slaves dropping by to pick up gallons of rum. Occasionally, the tapster noted the master's name; at other times he could not even identify the slave."[187]

"A WORSE EVIL HAS COME TO US"

The Reverend John R. Norwood, PhD (Kelekpethakomaxkw, "Smiling Thunderbear"), the pastor of Ujima Village Christian Church in Ewing Township, maintains an active ministry with the Nanticoke Lenni-Lenape Tribal Nation of Southern New Jersey. Norwood, during a November 2020 interview, said that during the colonial period, most of New Jersey's Lenape population had been pushed into Pennsylvania, "but there remained small communities in various New Jersey 'Indian Towns' and 'Indian Fields,' in addition to individual families that lived among colonists, adapting to colonial lifeways. Hunting territories were diminished and there were limits placed on free movement."

In 1756, West Jersey lawmakers and Nanticoke/Lenape leaders held a historic summit in the Burlington County town of Crosswicks to address grievances of the Indigenous people. Topics at the forum included access to hunting lands, the unrestricted passage of canoes and the selling of liquor to Native Americans—in private trading transactions and surreptitiously at taverns (despite the previously mentioned 1714 and 1751 legal decrees). A pamphlet, *A Treaty Between the Government of New Jersey and the Indians Inhabiting the Several Parts of Said Province*, records the proceedings of a meeting held on January 8 and 9, 1756.[188] New Jersey officials met with Cranberry, Pompton, Crosswicks and southern Jersey Native American representatives.

The Nanticoke-Lenape selected a spokesman named Ohiockechoque, who addressed the gathering on the morning of January 9, 1756. Norwood said the selection of Ohiockechoque indicated he had the confidence of the other tribal leaders and must have been a wise, strong defender of his people. "It was then, and remains now, a great honor and sign of deep trust to be selected to speak on behalf of tribal leaders." As recorded in the transcribed minutes of the meeting, Ohiockechoque spoke eloquently to the government representatives, an impassioned plea to stop the distribution of "strong liquor," presumably from taverns, which was fueling addiction among the Indigenous people of New Jersey:

The Reverend John R. Norwood. *Photo courtesy of Reverend Norwood.*

Sign for Nanticoke Lenni-Lenape Tribal Grounds, Bridgeton. *Photo by M. Gabriele.*

Dear brethren, some of our old men can remember when the English were weak and few, and the Indians strong and many. We then nursed them up in our bosoms and treated them as friends. We are glad our friendship hath continued so long and hope it will always endure. Since our fathers have sold so large a part of their lands to the English, we find it much more difficult to maintain ourselves and families by hunting, which is at least one half our support. But a worse evil than that has come to us, which is the use of strong liquor, to which the Indians are too much addicted…and for this, some of the English are too much to blame. We beg [that] you will take care to put a stop to this wicked practice. It may offend some of our foolish people at first, yet it will, at last, be best liked, and more for the health of soul and body.

In the afternoon session, the New Jersey representatives responded to the Native Americans:

We acknowledge the kindness your forefathers have shown to ours, and we shall always act kindly to you as we hope you will always deserve it, as long as the waters run down the Delaware. We are pleased to hear that you are sensible of the evils that arise by the too-great habit of drinking spirituous liquor among the Indians, and we shall lay that matter before the legislature of this province and shall endeavor to get a provision made against that evil.

Reverend Norwood pointed out that few historical voices of Native American people have been preserved from New Jersey's colonial days. After more than 265 years, Ohiockechoque's voice still resonates, documented in the 1756 pamphlet.

CHAPTER 4

TAVERNS IN THE TOWN

Fare thee well for I must leave thee
Do not let this parting grieve thee
And remember that the best of friends must part, must part
Adieu, adieu kind friends, adieu, yes adieu
I can no longer stay with you, stay with you
I'll hang my harp on a weeping willow tree
And may the world go well with thee

—lyrics from the song "There Is a Tavern in the Town"

STILL STANDING

Colonial taverns, as fixtures of communities, tracked the tempo of daily life in New Jersey. A handful of taverns from this period are still standing and serve as historic landmarks. Some have been or are being rebuilt. In many cases, the structures are long gone—their locations identified by roadside signposts—but their memories are preserved in out-of-print books and in the archives of libraries, museums and historical societies. Today, standing or not, they occupy an important place in the history of the state.

Tavern owners were entrepreneurs who had to earn public trust and maintain an honorable reputation in their business practices. On March 19, 1776, sixteen men went before a court session for the County of Gloucester

Barnsboro Inn, Sewell, Gloucester County. *Photo courtesy of Thomas Budd.*

to testify on behalf of John Barnes, who had applied for a tavern license. A statement by the men, inhabitants of the county, petitioned the court to approve a license for Barnes, stating that "an inn at this said house is much wanting." This petition, a formality during this era, assured the court that the license applicant would provide competent stewardship, maintain needed services and faithfully execute the role of tavern keeper.[189]

The structure, today known as the Barnsboro Inn, sits at the intersection of four roads in Sewell, a Mantua Township community in Gloucester County. The tavern's origins date back to 1740 or earlier, when John Budd built a log cabin on a stone foundation at the edge of a pine forest. British troops foraged through this part of Gloucester County in 1776 to 1779, "and doubtless the situation of the inn, atop the highest ground in the area, made it ideal for a lookout."[190] Thomas Budd, the current owner (who believes he's a descendant of John Budd), interviewed in July 2021, said there's a cut-out section in the tavern's wall that displays the structure's original logs.

The Black Horse Tavern, located at the corner of Mountain Avenue and Route 24/510 in Mendham, traces its origins to Ebenezer Byram (1692–1753), who came with his family to the village—known at the time as Roxiticus—from Bridgewater, Massachusetts, in the early 1740s. "In 1745 the people of Mendham began to build a new house of worship. Ebenezer Byram, prior to this, had built the Black Horse Tavern,

Black Horse Tavern, Mendham. *Photo by M. Gabriele.*

Gabreil Daveis Tavern, Gloucester Township. *Courtesy of John Brach, treasurer, Gloucester Township Historic and Scenic Preservation Committee.*

and the village had changed from Roxiticus (to Mendham). In 1740 there was only a bridle path or Indian trail between Roxiticus and West Hanover (Morristown)."[191]

Another living monument from the colonial era is the Gabreil Daveis Tavern, which is located in the Glendora section of Gloucester Township, Camden County, and maintained by the Gloucester Township Historic and Scenic Preservation Committee. John Brach, the treasurer with the committee, said a prominent colonial citizen, Gabreil Daveis, served as a town clerk, constable, tax collector and the overseer and surveyor of roads from 1747 to 1767 and built the eight-room tavern in 1756. He died in 1767, and his widow, Sarah, managed the tavern for two more years. Located along the Big Timber Creek and the old Irish Road, the tavern housed travelers and Patriot soldiers. The last private owner, William Schuck, who lived at the tavern from 1923 until he died in 1976, gifted the structure to Gloucester Township.[192]

THE CRANBURY EXPRESS

Beginning in 1716 and into the 1730s, the Middlesex County Legislature enacted bills to encourage stagecoach traffic from Burlington to Perth Amboy (a trip of about fifty miles), which offered ferry connections to and from Philadelphia and New York. The legislation sought to improve roadways, stimulate stagecoach competition and meet the growing demand to convey people and goods. "The journey required two days in the summer and three days in the winter; the cost of transportation to the traveler for a through passage was twenty shillings." A stage line established in 1766 promoted an innovation to enhance customer comfort: a coach with "springs on seats" for passengers.[193]

Stagecoaches passed through and stopped in Cranbury, creating business opportunities for taverns there. A newspaper advertisement, dated September 30, 1753, stated that "John Predmore and Daniel O'Bryan give notice that the stage from Perth Amboy will change horses and drivers at the house of John Predmore in Cranbury and proceed to Burlington on the same day."[194] John Predmore Jr. operated a posthouse on the site of the present Cranbury Inn. Richard Handley, who served in the Third Regiment Calvary Militia, established Handley's Tavern in 1780.[195] The tavern consisted of two posthouses on South Main Street. In 1800, newlyweds Peter Perrine and Hannah Disbrow Dey built their home "across the front of the two post

The Cranbury Inn, facing South Main Street, Cranbury. *Photo by M. Gabriele.*

houses." In later years, the houses became part of an expanded hotel, and in 1920, they were renamed the Cranbury Inn. "The inns of Cranbury evolved from Rescarrick's original rustic tavern [mentioned in chapter 1] to fancier establishments under John Predmore…and a long line of other successors in the town up to today's Cranbury Inn."[196]

Marching through Bernardsville

Following the Battle of Princeton on January 3, 1777, George Washington and the Continental army camped in Pluckemin for two days. Washington, in a letter to John Hancock, the president of the Continental Congress, wrote, "I have the honor to inform you…I have removed with the army under my command to this place [Pluckemin]. The difficulty of crossing the Delaware on account of the ice made our passage over it tedious." Washington ended the correspondence by informing Hancock that he planned to march his troops to Morristown, "where I shall endeavor to put them under the best cover I can; hitherto, we have been without any and many of our poor soldiers quite bare foot and ill clad in other respects."[197]

Fighting exhaustion and frigid winds, the general and his troops made their way to Morristown, a fifteen-mile trek that most likely followed a course similar to today's Route 202. On their way, they passed the John Parker Tavern in Bernardsville. Today, a stone on the front lawn of the

John Parker's Tavern, Bernardsville. *Photo courtesy of Pat Bankowski, Bernardsville Public Library.*

tavern, dedicated in January 1951 by the Daughters of the American Revolution, commemorates that journey, with the inscription: "By this route, Washington with his army retired to Morristown after his victory at Princeton, January 1777."

Captain John Parker of the First Battalion of Somerset County owned the tavern—which was built before 1750 and situated at the crossroads of today's Routes 202 and 525 in Bernardsville—and served the needs of Washington and his men during both Morristown encampments.[198] Originally from Perth Amboy, John Parker bought land in Bernardsville and acquired the tavern. The Continental army soldiers would have rubbed elbows with an assortment of regional characters, as this inn entertained a "diversified clientele with merchants, travelers and gentlemen." The John Parker Tavern also became the site of wartime intrigue. General Anthony Wayne met with soldiers on January 2, 1781, regarding claims for back pay and supplies. While staying at the tavern, Wayne was robbed of valuable dispatches. A British spy was hanged for the crime.[199]

Parker died at age thirty-three on March 4, 1781. The building operated as a tavern until 1840, when it became a private residence and a post office, and the area, once known as Vealtown, was renamed Bernardsville. Colonial Vealtown was settled in 1731 as a farming hamlet along Mine Brook stream. The Bernardsville Library Association acquired the tavern in 1990, and it's now used as a community center.

HERR MOELICH VISITS PLUCKEMIN

The story of Jacob Eoff's tavern reflects the formation of the village of Pluckemin in Bedminster Township, Somerset County, the founding of a historic Lutheran Church and the migration of German immigrants to New Jersey. Jacob Eoff, a prosperous farmer, purchased five hundred acres of land in Pluckemin, known as the Johnston estate, in 1741. Nine years later, Eoff established a stone tavern at the village crossroads in 1750.[200] As mentioned, Washington sent a letter to John Hancock on January 5, 1777, while stationed in Pluckemin. It's likely that Eoff provided food and drink to the weary Continental army soldiers at his tavern as they trudged to a winter encampment in Morristown.

Famine and European military conflicts triggered the 1709–10 Palatine Migration, when "as many as 30,000 German-speaking migrants left their homes, hoping for a better life in America." From this group, an estimated 3,000 landed in New York and Philadelphia, "representing the first substantial migration of German speakers to colonial America."[201] For those Germans who arrived in Philadelphia, many crossed the Delaware River into New Jersey and relocated to Long Valley, Oldwick and Pluckemin.[202]

A German immigrant named Johannes Moelich arrived in Philadelphia on September 28, 1733, having set sail from Rotterdam, the Netherlands. He came to New Jersey, and by 1750, he owned a large tract of land in Hunterdon County; he purchased additional property in Somerset County in 1751. In 1752, he rode through Pluckemin, "where the nucleus of a society was forming." Upon reaching Pluckemin, Herr Moelich found about a dozen small houses and Jacob Eoff's tavern. "This inn was the first place of entertainment established in the township....Jacob Eoff was one of the pioneers of the village. It is fair to presume that Johannes dismounted at Eoff's tavern to wish Jacob *guten morgen* [good morning] and discuss with him the quality of some of his best Jamaica [rum]."

The fifty-year-old Johannes Moelich had a striking appearance: a robust figure with blue eyes and an abundant reddish-brown beard. He dressed like a well-to-do yeoman of the era, with a coarse gray coat, a waistcoat and breeches made of leather, deerskin leggings extending over buckled shoes, a short gray wig and three-cornered hat and a pair of saddlebags suspended on either side of his horse.[203]

Eoff was a respected community leader and a member of the Lutheran church. He donated a portion of his land for the construction of a new

Neitzer's Tavern, Long Valley. *Photo by M. Gabriele.*

house of worship, Saint Paul's Lutheran Church. The cornerstone was laid on July 4, 1757. Following Jacob Eoff's death in 1780, "the tavern was kept for a short time by his maiden sister, Sarah. She, in turn, was succeeded by Jacob's son, Christian, who built a new tavern; a long, low building called the Barracks." A fire in 1814 destroyed the tavern.[204]

The Palatine Migration extended into today's Long Valley (previously known as German Valley) and the Schooley Mountain region of Morris County. Traveling from Philadelphia, the German immigrants "were so charmed by the rolling lands of Morris County that they quietly took possession."[205] Settlements and property purchases occurred during the 1740s, and a gristmill was established around 1767. Members of the Neitzer (Nitser) family became prominent in the community. John Peter Neitzer opened a general store in the village. He came from Wurttenberg (Wirtemberg), Germany, and arrived in Philadelphia on October 8, 1744. William Neitzer (Peter's nephew) became the first tavern keeper in the 1760s. Other tavern keepers followed William into the 1800s.[206] The two-story tavern structure still stands and today is part of Long Valley's Restaurant District.

WOOLVERTON'S STONE TAVERN

Colonial settlers reached the verdant hinterlands of the Minisink Valley in the mid-1600s. The valley, located in Sussex and Warren Counties, stretches along both sides of the Delaware River, from Port Jervis, New York, to the Delaware Water Gap.[207] Settlers included Huguenots, Dutch, Welsh, Quakers, Germans and Scotch/Irish, "with a considerable intermixture of the Puritans of New England, all noted for their struggles for civil and religious liberty in the European countries whence they came." Tribes of the Lenni-Lenape Nation lived in the region. The Old Mine Road, originally designed to support mining operations in the area, proved to be useful to settlers traveling from Upstate New York to the valley, "furnishing them with convenient access to their future homes in the wilderness."[208]

On November 20, 1753, the first court of justice in Sussex County met at Jonathan Pettit's tavern in Hardwick (today's Johnsonburg). The county court named commissioners and justices and appointed a sheriff and constable. The court also granted tavern licenses to seven men, including Pettit and a landowner named Thomas Woolverton, and affixed "the rates at which inn keepers should dispose of their liquors and provender." Two years later, the court tapped Woolverton as the county tax collector. In April 1754, another governing body, the Sussex County Board of Justices and Freeholders, met at the dwelling house of Samuel Green, and citizens petitioned to erect a "logg gaol" (jail), which would be paid for by the county. It was determined the jail would be built adjacent to Jonathan Pettit's tavern. The tavern and jail were located near the intersection of today's Routes 661 and 612 in Johnsonburg. A stone structure being used as a garage currently occupies the foundation of the old jail.[209] An ancient triangular milestone located outside the village has an inscription: "2 TO LG [two miles to Logg Gaol]." A historic marker reads: "Famous Milestone—A marker erected in 1754 to guide travelers on their way to the seat of Sussex County government at the Logg Gaol."

"The business of tavern keeping at this time was a stepping stone to public distinction, as well as a source of pecuniary profit. Nearly all early judges, justices, sheriffs and chosen freeholders were innkeepers." On September 3, 1750, Thomas Woolverton of Huntsville (today's Green Township) obtained a deed for ninety-one acres of property along the Pequest River. The property also included a sawmill, a gristmill and a forge to process iron from the nearby Andover mine. By 1756, meetings of the county court were transferred to Woolverton's stone tavern.[210] According to information posted

Above: Stone structure that occupies the foundation of the old Logg Gaol (jail) in Johnsonburg. *Photo by M. Gabriele.*

Left: Historic milestone, Logg Gaol, Johnsonburg, Sussex County. *Photo by M. Gabriele.*

Woolverton's Tavern historic marker, Green Township. *Photo by M. Gabriele.*

Thomas Woolverton's Tavern, Green Township (under construction). *Photo by M. Gabriele.*

on the historic marker on Pequest Road ("Thomas Woolverton's Tavern"), in 1755, Royal Governor Jonathan Belcher ordered that Sussex County's government and courts be moved to Woolverton's tavern. The transfer of court meetings occurred due to "disputes between county freeholders and Jonathan Pettit, who attempted to secure personal and economic benefit from locating the County Seat on his lands."

Debra Natyzak, the founder and president of the Frelinghuysen Township Historical Society, said Woolverton initially operated a tavern in Hardwick. He later built or acquired the stone tavern in Huntsville after getting the deed for the ninety-one acres of property. Natyzak, interviewed in July 2022, said the tavern, along with many other structures in the area, was constructed from Sussex County's natural limestone and most likely represents the masterful work of German stonemasons from that period. The Sussex County Board of Justices and Freeholders held its first meeting at Woolverton's tavern on May 12, 1756, and continued to gather there until 1762. By the mid-1770s, the Patriot movement, based in the town of Newton, had taken hold, and one thousand county residents, "interested in the independence of the colonies in the struggle for liberty," enlisted in the Continental army.[211] Woolverton died in the summer of 1759. Justices and freeholders met at the tavern on May 9, 1759, and then reconvened four months later at the "house of widow Woolverton," when they appointed a new county tax collector.[212]

Richard Vohden, the owner of Pequest Valley Farms in Green Township and a member of the Green Township Historical Society and the Sons of the American Revolution, said Woolverton's tavern was a stagecoach stop on the colonial highway that connected eastern Pennsylvania with Newark and New York. Vohden, who resides down the road from the stone tavern, said in a July 2022 interview that while Woolverton operated his tavern, his main interest in the property was the iron forge. A road trip to Green Township in July 2022 revealed that the stone tavern was undergoing renovation work.

FLOATING ALONG THE RANCOCAS CREEK

Mount Holly's four leading taverns prior to the Revolution were the Three Tuns, the Black Horse, the Cross Keys and Washington Tavern, according to historian George DeCou. Stagecoach travelers, along with farms and businesses in the area, supported these establishments. DeCou cited an article in the September 13, 1759 edition of the *Pennsylvania Gazette*, which stated that "a stage wagon was erected from Daniel Cooper's ferry [in Camden] to Mount Holly, thence through Monmouth County to Middletown. Daniel Jones, proprietor of Three Tuns Tavern, and Zachariah Rossell of the Black Horse were interested in this enterprise."[213] The Three Tuns Tavern (mentioned in chapter 3 and today known as the Mill Street Hotel and Tavern), still standing and located at the corner of Pine Street and Mill Street in Mount Holly, opened in 1731. (The Old English word *tun* referred to a liquid measurement of 250 gallons.)[214]

Barb Johns, president of the Mount Holly Historical Society, described the village as a colonial "market town," which benefitted from the conveyance of goods via the northern branch of the Rancocas Creek. This branch was part of the main Rancocas Creek, which connected with the Delaware River. The creek was navigable, according to Johns, interviewed in July 2022. The waterway powered Mount Holly's sawmill and gristmill operations. The village also had an ironworks and farms. All this local commerce accounted for the disposable income needed to support Mount Holly's thriving tavern scene. "The farmers came to Mount Holly [known at the time as Bridgetown] to sell their produce, and then spent their money at the Mount Holly taverns," Johns said.

Three Tuns Tavern/Mill Street Hotel, circa 1935. *Courtesy of Joanne M. Nestor, New Jersey State Archives, New Jersey Department of State.*

In June 1778, the British army marched through Mount Holly as part of its evacuation from Philadelphia and commandeered the Three Tuns Tavern. "It was clear in the early stages of the march that Mount Holly was the logical target as the small South Jersey town acted as a hub for the major road networks in the region. Mount Holly had served as the main American base of [military] operations."[215]

"During their brief stay at Mount Holly, [General Charles] Cornwallis and Hessian commander [Lieutenant General Wilhelm] van Knyphausen occupied rooms at a tavern [Three Tuns] on the main highway. This was the first hotel in Mount Holly. It stands in a part of the town around which all activities were centered." Cornwallis and Knyphausen rendezvoused in Mount Holly on June 20, 1778, and departed two days later.[216] Their subsequent maneuvers presaged the Battle of Monmouth on June 28, 1778, thirty-five miles northeast of Mount Holly.

POURING SHOTS FOR FURNACE WORKERS

Nestled at the intersection of Van Syckel (also spelled Van Syckle) and Charlestown Roads (Route 635) in Hampton is the Van Syckel Tavern, which was the favorite place of the men working at the nearby Union Furnace in the mid-1700s. Douglas D. Martin, the current occupant, said the stone building originally was known as Reynold's Tavern, built and operated by David Reynolds, a blacksmith at the furnace, along with a crew of fellow workers, around 1763. The tavern had three rooms, a loft for sleeping accommodations and separate structures for a kitchen and outbuilding.

A local historian and Van Syckel descendant, Martin, interviewed in November 2021, said local residents and Union Furnace employees patronized the tavern, which became a meeting hall for this farming region, known at the time as Bethlehem Township (today's Union Township). During the 1760s, Reynolds supported the cause of American independence and became a founding member of the Sons of Liberty chapter in Hunterdon County (see the Ringo's Tavern section in this chapter.) Reynolds also fell in with a group of counterfeiters. Producing counterfeit money was a serious crime during the colonial era. The British uncovered the scheme, and Reynolds was hanged in Morristown on September 17, 1773.[217]

Following the demise of David Reynolds, the tavern passed through various owners. Aaron Van Syckel bought the tavern and surrounding acreage in 1800. Van Syckel expanded the building and promoted the

Van Syckel's Tavern, Union Township, Hunterdon County. *Photo by M. Gabriele.*

tavern as a stagecoach stop. By the early 1900s, the tavern was shuttered and remained unoccupied for many years. Martin arrived on the scene in 2001 and restored the building in order to preserve it. A year later, he reopened the tavern to visitors. He's resided at the old tavern as a family representative since 2020.

William Honachefsky Jr., an author and vice president of the Union Forge Heritage Association, interviewed in December 2021, said that Philadelphia business partners William Allen and Joseph Turner established the Union Furnace near Reynold's Tavern in 1742. Martin said Allen and Turner wanted the tavern for the benefit of their workers. By 1775, the business had evolved into the Union Iron Works and produced cannonballs for the Continental army.

"All Roads Led to Woodbridge"

On April 16, 1789, George Washington and his entourage departed from Mount Vernon, Virginia, for a triumphant 240-mile journey to Federal Hall in New York City, where he was to be inaugurated as president of the United States on April 30, 1789.[218] Author Donald Johnstone Peck writes that

Washington passed through Princeton and New Brunswick, and on April 22, he arrived in Woodbridge and spent the night at the Cross Keys Tavern.

> *The Cross Keys Tavern had been a cradle of the revolt. It was the headquarters for revolution in Woodbridge and a popular rallying place for the Sons of Liberty to discuss their grievances. Travelers had brought news of similar ferment in other colonies, petitions were drawn up and signed, tea boycotts were organized and militia units had been formed. Seditious talk in the Cross Keys' smoky taproom would have given the* [General Joseph] *Bloomfield men of Woodbridge quite a bit to discuss at their dinner tables.*[219]

The term *cross keys* refers to an important crossroads in a village. John Manning, Woodbridge's first postmaster, built the Cross Keys in 1740.[220] Originally located at the intersection of Main Street and Perth Amboy Avenue, the tavern was relocated to North James Street in the 1920s.[221]

The British settled Woodbridge in 1665, with a charter granted on June 1, 1669. In June 1683, the Woodbridge court selected Samuel Moore to keep the first tavern.[222] Woodbridge historian Amy E. Breckenridge described Samuel Moore as "one of the town's most distinguished citizens, and no one

Cross Keys Tavern, Woodbridge. *Photo by M. Gabriele.*

was better known or more implicitly trusted." The tavern stood at the corner of Green Street and Rahway Avenue.[223]

"Colonial Woodbridge had a choice of taverns dotting the thoroughfares, ready to serve civic affairs and wayward travelers alike," historian Doug Wilson writes. "Woodbridge, strategically located near ferry docks across the rivers and bays from New York and on the most direct path to Philadelphia, saw its share of travelers." The Elm Tree Tavern, located on Turnpike Road/ Rahway Avenue, was a popular establishment in Woodbridge, according to Wilson. He said James Jr. and Mary (Fitz Randolph) Jackson were the proprietors of the Elm Tree from 1739 to 1759—so named because of a massive elm tree on the property.[224]

"All colonial New Jersey roads led to Woodbridge," Wendi Rottweiler, local history librarian at the Woodbridge Public Library, said in an October 2021 interview. "The Minisink and Assunpink trails of the Lenni-Lenape developed into wagon roads. Royal post roads connected colonial settlements, and the navigable waterways of the Raritan River, Arthur Kill and Papiack [Woodbridge] Creek linked Woodbridge to other East Coast ports. Patriot groups such as the Jersey Blues, Sons of Liberty and Middlesex Militia traveled to Woodbridge, planning local defenses and fomenting revolution in the village taverns."

"A Man of Consequence in the Community"

On Saturday, August 27, 1774, John Adams—the future vice president and president of the United States—made an entry into his diary as he approached the campus of "Prince Town," known at the time as the College of New Jersey. "This whole colony of New Jersey is a *champaign* [an expanse of open country]. About 12 o'clock we arrived at the tavern in Prince Town, which holds out the 'Sign of Hudibras,' near Nassau Hall College. The tavern keepers' name is [Jacob] Hyer." Later that afternoon, Adams joined the college president, John Witherspoon, for a glass of wine at Princeton's Maclean House. "The government of this college is very strict and the scholars study very hard. The president says they are all Sons of Liberty."[225] As a delegate from Massachusetts, Adams passed through New Jersey on his way to the first Continental Congress held in Philadelphia, which opened on September 5, 1774. Delegates initially gathered at City Tavern and then walked to Carpenters Hall.[226]

Interpretive drawing of the Hudibras Tavern by artist Gus Escher. *Courtesy of Gus Escher; for a July 1983* Princeton Packet *article by Connie Escher.*

Jacob Hyer took ownership of the Hudibras in June 1768. He previously had been the innkeeper at Princeton's King's Arms Tavern. A businessman named George Campbell purchased the Sign of the Hudibras from a certain Mr. Yard in 1761. Yard erected the Hudibras in the early 1750s. By 1765, Campbell was looking to sell the place. "This last owner had no joy of the place, for after four years of residence, his liabilities assumed proportions that demanded the sale of the house."[227]

Campbell described the features of the tavern and its surrounding property in the May 16, 1765 edition of the *New York Gazette or Weekly Post Boy*:[228]

To be sold either at public or private sale, the noted and well-accustomed tavern, the Hudibras at Prince-Town. It is esteemed by all gentlemen acquainted with the road, to be the best stand between New York and Philadelphia. The house is new, has a cellar under the whole and has twelve rooms; two good kitchens, one of which has a loft over it with two good rooms; a good stable with a large loft which will hold five tons of hay;

two sheds, a large boarded barrack, a large hen house, a hog house and a new hen coop two-stories high, which will contain two-hundred fowls. There is a small lot of ground and adjoining it two excellent gardens well stored with greens, salads, herbs and all sort of garden stuff. Also to be sold, a servant girl who understands all sorts of house work and has three years to serve.

Hyer achieved the rank of lieutenant colonel in the Third Middlesex Militia while he owned the Hudibras. "Hyer was every inch a colonel. He was a good church member, a thorough Patriot and an ideal citizen. To the cause of freedom he gave generously, and offered his life in the forefront of the fight. Students and professors found him a man ever ready to help a friend in need with kind sympathy and a timely loan. He was no low bar keeper, but an esteemed citizen; a man of consequence in the community."[229]

An essay from the archives of the Historical Society of Princeton indicates that roast beef and rabbit stew were the most popular offerings at the Hudibras—cooked throughout the day in the tavern's separate outbuilding kitchen and served with bread and cheese. Hyer's alcohol stash included Madeira and claret wine, porter, gin, cider and cherry whiskey. Dessert featured honey cakes, fruits, nuts and wine. Hyer also offered customers long clay pipes for an after-dinner smoke.

The kitchens of "upscale" colonial village taverns might have looked like this recreated kitchen at Ford Mansion, Washington's Headquarters, Morristown. *Photo by M. Gabriele.*

A blaze in the early morning hours of January 22, 1773, gutted the Hudibras, as reported in the February 1, 1773 edition of the *Pennsylvania Packet*. The newspaper reprinted a letter, dated January 23, 1773, which provided an eyewitness account of the incident:[230]

Yesterday morning [January 22] *between three and four o'clock, I was awakened by the cry of fire: I immediately arose, and having dressed myself, hastened out and enquired where the fire was; I was informed it was at the house of Mr. Jacob Hyer, at the Sign of Hudibras. I ran immediately to the place, and found the northeast corner in flames. The college fire engine and buckets being brought, all possible means were used to extinguish the flames, but to no purpose; the fire burned till seven o'clock, when the whole house was laid in ashes. Mr. Hyer lost all his winter provisions, beds and other furniture. The students upon this occasion behaved with a becoming boldness, which does them honor. 'Tis to be hoped this accident will cause people to be careful in putting out their candles before they go to sleep.*

Hyer rebuilt the tavern and reopened in November 1773, as reported in the November 15, 1773 edition of the *Pennsylvania Chronicle*. "The noted inn, at the Sign of the Hudibras at Princeton, New Jersey, is again opened where it was formerly kept, by Jacob Hyer, who hath made ample provision for the reception and entertainment of travelers and others. And as he hath ever exerted himself to oblige, he hopes he shall meet with future marks of public favor."[231]

The tavern's name, Hudibras, came from the title of a burlesque satirical poem written by English author Samuel Butler and published during the 1660s and 1670s. In the poem, Butler mocked what he saw as the pretentiousness and hypocrisy in militant Puritanism of his era, with the hero of the poem, Hudibras, portrayed as a cowardly, bumbling knight.[232]

Born in New Brunswick on October 5, 1736, Jacob Hyer died in Princeton on August 27, 1785, according to the Historical Society of Princeton's archives. Following Hyer's demise, various new owners renamed the tavern the Red Lion and the City Hotel; Princeton razed the structure in the late 1860s or early 1870s. On April 24, 1969, construction began on an addition to Princeton's Harvey S. Firestone Memorial Library, which occupies the Hudibras's footprint. Prior to the start of the library's construction, the Historical Society of Princeton, supported by the university, conducted an archaeological project known as the Hudibras Tavern Dig and organized an exhibit from April to September 1970, displaying fragments of plates, pottery and glass.

Another tavern keeper, William Hick, arrived in Princeton from Philadelphia in 1763 and four years later became manager of the Sign of the College Tavern. The establishment served as a stagecoach stop for John Barnill's Flying Machine route between New York and Philadelphia. The tavern hosted meetings of college and town organizations, and on September 30, 1772, Hick welcomed college trustees, who ran up a tab that included sixty dinners, twelve double bowls of punch, seventeen bottles of beer, twenty-one bottles of Madeira wine and six bowls of rum toddy. Despite the tavern's success, the political environment of Princeton was hostile to Hick's outspoken views as a Loyalist. By the end of 1773, "matters had gone far enough on the Princeton campus to make the village uncomfortable for a Loyalist Englishman with a careless tongue. Hick was virtually driven out of Princeton for his pro-British sentiments."[233]

Having worn out his welcome, Hick posted an ad in *Dunlap's Pennsylvania Packet* newspaper, dated February 7, 1774, that announced he was leaving Princeton and that he had taken over the Sign of the King's Arms Tavern in Perth Amboy.[234] Two years after arriving in Perth Amboy, Hick's life took a tragic turn. The colonial militia arrested Hick and jailed him in Trenton. Officials granted him permission to return to England, but he died in 1780 during the passage across the ocean.[235]

"WINE AND ARGUMENTS FLOWED FREELY"

In October 1945, the editors of the *Princeton Alumni Weekly* published a remembrance feature about the idyllic days of carousing at Princeton's old Nassau Inn during the mid-1700s. "While many of our members will doubtless recall the 'Old Nass' on account of it being a rendezvous where generations of college boys have drunk their beer and sung their songs, few are familiar with it having been a famous tavern as far back as in pre-Revolutionary days." The article describes the tavern as being "the center of the town's life [where] taproom wine and arguments flowed freely." New Jersey's Committee of Safety met at the Old Nass in 1775, and delegates to the First Continental Congress in Philadelphia stopped for the night, as well as signers of the Declaration of Independence while passing through Princeton. When the Revolutionary War began, "military men stopped here at intervals. Officers of the Continental army, likewise British and Hessians, halted to enjoy the facilities of the taproom." The article also mentions Princeton lore, saying that students, faculty and townspeople came to the tavern to "listen to news and opinions of out-of-town guests" such as Paul Revere and Thomas Paine.[236]

Thomas Leonard arrived in Princeton around 1710, relocating from Massachusetts, and soon was lauded as a wealthy, generous landowner, providing a major donation to the College of New Jersey (Princeton). Leonard served as a judge and a member of the colonial legislature in Somerset County. In 1756, he built an elegant residence at 52 Nassau Street in Princeton "of brick imported by him from Holland."[237] Leonard died in 1759, and his home became the Nassau Inn, known locally under different names such as the Sign of the College or the College Inn, with Christopher Beekman as the first proprietor. "Here the trustees of the college held their generous commencement dinners, until the Revolution and rising prices broke up the custom. The building was seriously damaged by fire in 1925, and in 1937 was torn down to make way for Palmer Square. Reminders of jovial evenings at the Old Nass have been transferred to the Yankee Doodle Taproom of the new Nassau Tavern in Palmer Square."[238]

"A Sweet, Wholesome and Delightful Place"

In May 1776, George and Martha Washington made plans to travel to Philadelphia from New York City. An expense account reveals the movements of George and Martha. They began their trip by ferryboat from New York on May 21 and were entertained at Hick's Tavern in Perth Amboy. The Washingtons passed through New Brunswick, Princeton and Trenton, stopping at taverns, before reaching Philadelphia.[239] On May 23, 1776, a Philadelphia newspaper reported on their arrival. "Thursday afternoon, about two o'clock, his excellency General Washington arrived in this city from New York." The next day, Washington met with a committee appointed by Congress.[240]

The Perth Amboy tavern keeper was William Hick, who previously managed the Sign of the College Tavern in Princeton, as mentioned earlier. Historian and author Donald Peck and John Kerry Dyke, Perth Amboy city historian, said the King's Arms, located on the northwest corner of High and Smith Streets, later became known as the Hotel Packer or Packer House. A fire on March 17, 1969, gutted the historic structure.

Dyke pointed out it isn't clear where the Washingtons would have spent the night in Perth Amboy or at various points on their journey. "It has been assumed by modern people that George and Martha Washington did what people do nowadays—that is, stay in hotels," he wrote to this author in a July 2021 email. "During colonial days, men traveling with their wives typically stayed in the private residences of friends, family or gentry."

Perth Amboy can trace its origins to deeds written in the mid-1600s, in which it's referred to as Emboyle and Amboyle and, later, as "Ambo Point." The early proprietors had designated Perth Amboy as the capital of East Jersey, and a proposal they wrote laid out their ambitious vision "to erect and build one principal town…to be placed upon a neck or point of rich land, lying on the Raritan River…where ships in that great harbor commonly rise at anchor. For as much as Amboy Point is a sweet, wholesome and delightful place, proper for trade by reason of its commodious situation upon a safe harbor, being likewise accommodated with a navigable river and fresh water, and [has] by many persons of the greatest experience and best judgment, been approved for the goodness of the air, soil and situation. We the proprietors purpose by help of Almighty God, with all convenient speed, to build a convenient town for merchandise, trade and fishery."[241]

Perth Amboy would have provided abundant business opportunities for tavern keepers during this period. Author William Whitehead identified the Long Ferry Tavern as Perth Amboy's first "public house," built in 1684,

Long Ferry Tavern, Perth Amboy. *Photo courtesy of John Kerry Dyke, Perth Amboy Historian.*

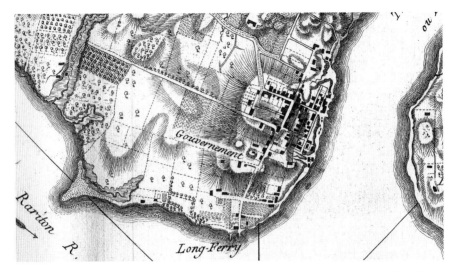

Map of southern tip of Perth Amboy, 1776, showing location of the Long Ferry Slip. *Photo courtesy of John Kerry Dyke, Perth Amboy Historian.*

"where grey-beard mirth and smiling toil retired, and village statesmen talked with looks profound."[242] Dyke said Perth Amboy had two ferry slips during the eighteenth century. One was at the foot of High Street, known as the Long Ferry Dock, at the southern tip of Perth Amboy. This was the ferry slip that transported people and freight across Raritan Bay to South Amboy. Adjacent to this ferry slip was the Long Ferry Tavern, which burned down in 1867. "This tavern was a hot spot during the American Revolution," Dyke said. "British and American forces used the Long Ferry slip and its tavern." Perth Amboy's other ferry slip was located at the end of Dock Street (currently named Fayette Street) along the banks of the Arthur Kill waterway.

Dyke explained that, from 1721 to 1769, the colony of New Jersey charged no tariffs on slave ships. As a result, Perth Amboy became a major importer of enslaved people, initially from the Caribbean Islands of Barbados and Montserrat and later directly from West Africa. "In the years that followed, the mindset changed in Perth Amboy. During the mid-nineteenth century, Perth Amboy became a major station of the Underground Railroad movement [the secret network of safe houses that aided escaped enslaved people]. From the Eagleswood site in Perth Amboy, countless numbers of people were sent to freedom. The good people of Perth Amboy transformed their hometown from a port of slavery to a port of freedom."

"A Beautiful Rainbow and Excellent Grog"

Abraham Godwin opened his Passaic Hotel and Tavern, which was located on River Street at the foot of Bank Street in Paterson, in the summer of 1774. Author Charles A. Shriner referred to the tavern as the most famous of ancient houses in Paterson. Shriner described the ancient dwellings "as being generally of one type—long and low, seldom more than one-story in height, with gambrel roofs rising high up in the air. These houses were erected to stand for generations."[243]

Announcing the start of his business, Godwin, a carpenter, posted a newspaper ad, saying he had "lately built a new and very commodious house for tavern keeping," which included dining, drinking, and lodging, "with the best accommodation for horses. A convenient room for dancing, and a fiddler, will always be ready for the services of ladies and gentlemen who may require it." Also provided would be "a guide to attend any strangers who shall show them all the natural curiosities at the falls."[244]

The "falls" in the advertisement refers to the Great Falls of Paterson and indicates Godwin was well aware of the advantages of his surroundings in marketing his tavern for colonial tourists. Alexander Hamilton, George

Historic plaque, Abraham Godwin, East Side Park, Paterson. *Photo by M. Gabriele.*

Paterson Great Falls National Historical Park. *Photo by M. Gabriele.*

Washington, the Marquis de Lafayette and James McHenry were among the tourists who visited the Great Falls on Friday, July 10, 1778.[245] McHenry, who served as a surgeon in the Continental army and was an advisor to Washington, penned an account of the visit in his journal, writing that the army was on its way to Paramus and camped near the Great Falls "in order to rest and refresh." Based on McHenry's account, the four men enjoyed a picnic and conversation:[246]

> *When I returned to the encampment, I found the general and suite seated under a large spreading oak within view of the spray* [from the falls], *diversified by a beautiful rainbow. The traveling canteens were immediately emptied and a modest repast spread before us, of cold ham, tongue and some biscuit. With the assistance of a little spirit, we composed some excellent grog* [rum]. *Then we chatted away a very cheerful half hour and then took our leave of the friendly oak.*

Inspired by the cordial gathering and perhaps a few swigs of grog, Hamilton envisioned Paterson as an industrial center. After being appointed the first secretary of the treasury, he developed a plan to start an industrial revolution in the United States, which evolved into the Society for Establishing Useful

Alexander Hamilton statue, Great Falls National Park, Paterson. *Photo by M. Gabriele.*

Manufactures, a state-sponsored corporation.[247] Throughout the 1800s and into the early 1900s, the Great Falls powered silk mills, which earned Paterson the nickname Silk City. On November 7, 2011, the National Park Service dedicated the Great Falls as the United States's 397th National Park.[248] Today, a statue of Hamilton faces the seventy-foot-high waterfalls.

DECLARING INDEPENDENCE IN NEW BRUNSWICK

New Brunswick was a stop on the "well-traveled post roads" and stagecoach lines that connected New York and Philadelphia. To accommodate the many travelers, "a multiplicity of houses of entertainment [taverns] in New Brunswick was the necessary result of these conditions. Among the various inns: the Red Lion, the Unicorn, the Padlock, the Tree of Liberty, the Ship, and the Indian Queen."[249]

Pehr (Peter) Kalm, a celebrated botanist, explorer and scholar, wrote about life in New Brunswick in the late 1740s. The Swedish Academy of Sciences commissioned Kalm to travel to North America "for the purpose of describing the natural productions of that part of the world and of introducing from thence into Sweden such useful plants as might be expected to thrive in the north of Europe." On August 5, 1748, he set out from the seaport town of Gravesend, in the county of Kent, England, and arrived in Philadelphia on September 15, 1748. Kalm spent several weeks in Pennsylvania and then began his journey through New Jersey, visiting New Brunswick on October 29, 1748, which he described as

> *a pretty little town in a valley on the west side of the river Rareton* [Raritan]. *The greater part of all* [New Brunswick's] *trade is to New York. To that place they send corn, flour in great quantities, bread, several other necessities, a great quantity of linseed, boards, timber, wooden vessels, and all sorts of carpenter's work. The inhabitants, likewise, get a considerable profit from travelers* [presumably those stopping at taverns], *who every hour pass through on the high road.*[250]

The "lost" river port of Raritan Landing, located along the Raritan River and today's Johnson Park in Piscataway and Highland Park, was a settlement that dates to the early 1700s but was dismantled and forgotten by the end of the nineteenth century, according to historian and archaeologist Rebecca Yamin. The community consisted of a cluster of houses, stores and at least one tavern. Raritan Landing was rediscovered in the 1970s and 1980s through a series of construction projects as well as digs organized by the Rutgers Archaeological Survey Office. Research done by Joel Grossman at that office indicated Raritan Landing "was an important commercial center for the cargo sloops that sailed the coast of the colonies" and served as a port that received shipments of knives, ceramics, clothing, books, pewter, stoneware and earthenware, all of which were sold by local merchants. Artifacts and building foundations were later discovered during the 2008 expansion of Rutgers University's football stadium.[251]

Yamin writes that the Rising Sun Tavern operated among the shopkeepers at Raritan Landing and was frequented by seamen delivering cargo. The tavern might have opened as early as 1733, run by tavern keepers Abraham Lane and George Vroom. However, in 1756, the minutes of the Court of Common Pleas for Middlesex County noted that there was "a recommendation in honor of Abraham Lane Esquire for a license to keep a tavern in the house where he now lives at the Landing." The tavern closed around 1846.[252] The Cornelius Low House, built in 1741, is one of the last remaining structures of Raritan Landing. Low was a wealthy merchant and prospered at the river port. Today, the Low House serves as the Middlesex County Museum.

Cornelius Low House, Piscataway. *Photo by M. Gabriele.*

Colonel John Neilson of the Second Regiment of the Middlesex County militia gave one of the first public readings of the Declaration of Independence on July 9, 1776, in New Brunswick at a tavern on Albany Street, believed to have been the White Hall Tavern.[253] The Declaration of Independence was printed in Philadelphia by John Dunlap, and the Continental Congress ordered copies to be distributed to state assemblies, conventions, committees of safety and commanding officers of the Continental troops.[254] Congress sent a copy to Colonel Neilson, an outspoken opponent of British taxes. According to Neilson's obituary published in New York's *Evening Post*, he was well known by the Continental Congress. New Brunswick organized a gathering of citizens to hear Neilson publicly read the proclamation. "Fearless of personal consequences, Colonel Neilson ascended a stage hastily prepared for the occasion [most likely, a table from White Hall tavern], and with a firm and audible voice proceeded to read the Declaration to the assembled multitude. At the conclusion, he was greeted with loud huzzahs by so great a majority that the opponents of the measure did not dare to avow themselves."[255]

White Hall Tavern, established in the early 1750s, was a popular meeting place in New Brunswick due to the grain trade, so it would have been a logical choice for Neilson as a spot to attract a large audience. Grain and flour arrived by Conestoga wagons and cargo sloops navigating the Raritan River from farms throughout the Delaware Valley.

> *The grain business of New Jersey was carried on largely in New Brunswick, where cash was paid for the merchandise, as distinguished from Newark and Philadelphia, where barter was used. The White Hall Tavern was headquarters for news for these merchants, where they would congregate to get* [newspapers from New York]. *They would then agree among themselves as to the price to be paid for grain and thus make the market.*[256]

A public event on July 9, 2017, at the corner of George Street and Livingston Avenue, with eighteen descendants of the Neilson family on hand, unveiled a statue of Colonel Neilson—a full-circle moment that spanned 241 years and connected the past and present.[257] Susan Kramer-Mills, a board member of the New Brunswick Public Sculpture Committee, interviewed at the event, said that "art has the power to inspire, motivate and educate. Thus, with the sculpture of Colonel John Neilson, we celebrate the richness of our city's history with the hope that it will inspire, motivate and educate the generations to come."[258]

Colonel John Neilson statue, New Brunswick, created by sculptors Anna Koh Varilla and Jeffrey H. Varilla. *Photo by M. Gabriele.*

Drama at the Ligonier

The Continental Congress moved into the French Arms Tavern in Trenton on November 1, 1784, and was in session there until December 24, 1784, relocating from Annapolis, Maryland. The tavern was located at the southwest corner of today's Warren and State Streets, built of stone and stucco, two stories high, with a gabled roof. This was the period prior to Washington, D.C., being selected as the permanent capital of the new nation. From June to November 1783, Nassau Hall in Princeton also served as a temporary seat for the Continental Congress.[259]

The French Arms, erected around 1730, originally was a private residence. The structure was sold several times until April 1, 1780, when it was leased to Jacob G. Bergen and became a tavern. "Bergen was a Princetonian who had operated the College of Princeton Inn." Bergen named the tavern Thirteen Stars and did extensive remodeling: adding a third story, converting two first-floor rooms into a single "long room" and installing a barroom in the basement. The tavern was renamed French Arms to honor France's role in the Revolutionary War. Over the next seven years, there were additional ownership changes at the tavern, renamed the Blazing Star and then the City Tavern. On December 18, 1787, the tavern became the site for New Jersey's ratification of the United States Constitution—the third state to do so. In 1836, First Mechanics and Manufacturers Bank purchased the property, tore down the tavern and erected an office building.[260]

On February 4, 1754, Doctor Thomas Cadwalader (1707–1779), a physician, Patriot and Trenton landowner, "conveyed" his property at the corner of Broad and State Streets to James Rutherford. It was a two-story brick building with multiple rooms, a good cellar, a stone kitchen, a garden and stables, "situated in a very public part of the town of Trenton, very convenient for any public business." Five years later, James Rutherford conveyed the building to his nephew, Robert Rutherford, a tavern keeper. Robert Rutherford turned the corner brick house into the Ligonier or Black Horse Tavern.

Robert Rutherford faced considerable drama in his life. His youngest daughter, Frances Mary, abruptly ran off with a British officer, Colonel Fortescue, and the two fled to Paris. In 1765, Rutherford landed in prison because of debt. The Trenton court released him on November 27, 1766, and he continued to manage the Ligonier Tavern, but he still had financial woes. Samuel Tucker, the sheriff of Hunterdon County, posted a notice in the November 29, 1764 edition of the *Pennsylvania Gazette* advertising that the tavern was for sale. Funds raised through the sale of the tavern presumably would have been used to compensate creditors, who had filed a lawsuit. One of the creditors purchased the tavern in March 1767, and the following year, new ownership recast the Ligonier as the Royal Oak Tavern.[261] The curious name "Ligonier" refers to an elite regiment in the British army led by John Ligonier, a celebrated field marshal and colonel. Robert Rutherford had enlisted and served in Ligonier's army unit. He came to America and named his tavern in honor of Ligonier.[262]

A landowner and businessman named William Yard built the city's first inn, established sometime between 1712 and 1715 and known only through collective memory as William Yard's Inn. (It's plausible he may have been the same Mr. Yard mentioned in the Princeton section of this chapter.) By 1715, he had established a public house, described by the Trenton Historical Society as a "substantial stone dwelling," which stood at East Front Street, near the Old Barracks.[263] Yard, born near Exeter, Devonshire, England, came to the colonies in 1688 and first settled in Philadelphia. He relocated to Trenton in 1700, purchased two acres of land on what is now State Street and bought other large tracts of land. In 1719, the Hunterdon County Court met at Yard's Trenton tavern. Yard's will is dated February 14, 1742.[264]

Reconnaissance at Robins Tavern

Monmouth County taverns were in the thick of political and military activities during the Garden State's colonial and Revolutionary War years. Catherine (Applegate) Hart inherited Hart's Tavern in Colts Neck (today the site is occupied by the Colts Neck Inn) from her late husband, Levi Hart. Catherine married Hart in December 1757, when she was around age twenty-five. Born in England circa 1715, Hart came to America in 1737, settled in the Colts Neck area of Monmouth County and established himself as a successful tavern owner and merchant. He was one of many Jewish settlers who came to this part of Monmouth County during the early 1700s.[265] Levi Hart died in 1775, and an inventory of his estate found sizable quantities of porter, wine, brandy and rum at his tavern.[266]

Three years after Hart's death, Catherine married Patriot militia captain and privateer Joshua Huddy. Huddy earned a reputation as a fearless enemy of the British and had numerous legal disputes with Monmouth County Loyalists. Loyalists captured Huddy in Toms River in March 1782, and he was hanged on April 12, 1782.[267] A British magazine published an account

Gravestone of Joshua Huddy, Old Tennent Cemetery, Manalapan Township. *Photo by M. Gabriele.*

of his execution: "Captain Huddy was hanged at Middletown Point on the Rebel Jersey shore on the forenoon of the twelfth of April [1782] by way of retaliation for the murders which he and the Jersey Rebels committed." From the British perspective, the execution was revenge against Huddy and his Patriot followers for the "cruelties" they inflicted on Loyalists.[268]

The Taylor family, around 1727, established a residence and a separate large inn, "long known as the Old Tavern," in Middletown. Edward Taylor, Esquire (1712–1783), managed the family's Old Tavern. "Edward Taylor was an active, intelligent man, possessed of a liberal education. In 1768, 1772 and 1774 he was a member of the [Monmouth County] assembly." In the buildup to the Revolutionary War, Edward supported Boston Patriots in their effort to fight "taxation without representation," but this "activity gained him [the] animosity of his Tory neighbors."[269]

As a tavern owner and political leader, Taylor dealt with personal conflicts regarding the cause for independence. "At the beginning of the American Revolution, he supported the Patriots' cause by sending supplies to people in Boston. When his son, George, became a colonel in the British army, Taylor became sympathetic to the Loyalists' cause. He was put under house arrest at his home in Middletown. His neighbors suspected that he was a British spy who had given information to his son."[270] Taylor navigated through the controversies and left a large estate to his descendants.

The Village Inn Tavern, still standing and located at the intersection of Main and Water Streets in Englishtown, is recognized as the headquarters for General Washington during the Battle of Monmouth on June 28, 1778. Much of the Village Inn's fame stems from local history and oral tradition, along with letters penned and received by Washington on June 30, 1778. The letters were dated "headquarters Englishtown" and "camp Englishtown" but contained no precise location.[271] "Near the end of June 1778, before and after the Battle of Monmouth, it is likely that George Washington spent time at the two-and-a-half story Village Inn."[272]

The Historic American Buildings Survey reported that "the Village Inn has been prominent in local tradition as the place where George Washington

Village Inn Tavern, Englishtown. *Photo by M. Gabriele.*

stayed during the Battle of Monmouth, June 27–30, 1778. Research conducted in conjunction with the Historic Structures report, prepared in 1982, disclosed no documentary evidence to support this legend, nor any to contradict it." The conductors of the survey estimated that the structure was built in 1732 and went on to say that the inn "is significant in itself as an additive structure, reflecting various building traditions and styles from the eighteenth through the early twentieth century. Of particular note are the Dutch framing techniques, which were employed pre-1750." A local tailor, Robert Newell, owned the property, according to a 1726 deed, and erected the building. Newell sold the property to Thomas Davis in 1749, marking the start of the tavern business. Other owners followed Davis, and they continued to operate the Village Inn as a tavern. Six years after the inn was added to the National Register of Historic Places in 1972, the Battleground Historical Society purchased and restored the building. Today, the Village Inn serves as the headquarters for the society and is used as a museum.[273]

Gary D. Saretzky, Monmouth County archivist, in the catalogue for the October 2018 *Buildings in Monmouth: Stories and Styles* exhibit, cites Robins Tavern in Clarksburg, Millstone Township, as an "unsung place that played a brief role in history, then retreated into obscurity…an important landmark during the British and American maneuvers before the Battle

Robins Tavern was located in the village of Clarksburg, Millstone Township. Photo by Laura V. Stewart, May 1899. *Photo courtesy of Doreen Polhemus, Millstone Township historian.*

of Monmouth." It was known by various names over the years: it was Robins Tavern after it was purchased by Leonard Robins and the Willow Tree Tavern during the nineteenth century, while the British called it the Rising Sun Tavern. Saretzky explained that while most farmhouses in this region "were oriented southward to capture the warmth of the mid-day sun, this tavern faced easterly, to optimize the morning sunlight through the windows."[274]

Robins Tavern sat at the intersection of Routes 571 and 524/ Stagecoach Road (known in the 1700s as Old Shrewsbury Road). John Leming owned and perhaps built the tavern going back as far as 1745. James Debow purchased the tavern at a 1769 sheriff's sale and, six years later, sold it to Leonard Robins. A listing of tavern licenses granted by the Monmouth County Court of General Quarter Sessions on April 1775—preserved in the Monmouth County Archives—includes a license granted to Leonard Robins. One year earlier, Robins had purchased a farm on Route 524. Historian Robert W. Craig offers a "spare profile" of Leonard Robins, describing him as a man who worked to maintain the tavern business but "never prospered at it." He served in the Second Regiment of the Monmouth Militia, commanded by Colonel Samuel

Forman. Robins purchased rum, wheat, rye, corn, flour and oats from a Monmouth County merchant named William Tapscott. "Robins was three times fined for selling liquor in wholesale quantities, which tavern keepers were not allowed by law to do, and the fines became increasingly stiff." In 1781, Tapscott sued Robins due to the size of the unpaid tab he had accumulated, and the lawsuit marked the end of Robins's ownership of the tavern.[275]

In the prelude to the Battle of Monmouth, Alexander Hamilton, the Marquis de Lafayette and a corps of 1,500 troops reached Cranbury on the evening of June 25, 1778. Sometime before midnight, Hamilton left Lafayette and rode to Robins Tavern to do reconnaissance on British forces. The next morning at dawn, Lafayette and his light infantry left Cranbury and joined Hamilton at Robins Tavern, which Lafayette used as his field outpost. On June 26, 1778, Washington and the main body of the Continental army reached Cranbury and made plans to confront the British.[276]

Hamilton and Lafayette joined forces with Washington for the Battle of Monmouth on June 28, 1778. Craig noted the importance of Robins Tavern as "a crucial marker to reconstruct the maneuvers and encounters that the British and Continental armies underwent before the battle." He wrote that

Monmouth Battlefield State Park, 2022 reenactment event. *Photo courtesy of James Douglas, New Jersey Department of Environmental Protection.*

1778 ☀ 1901
IN GRATEFUL REMEMBRANCE
OF PATRIOTS WHO, ON SABBATH JUNE 28, 1778,
GAINED THE VICTORY WHICH WAS THE TURNING POINT
IN THE WAR FOR INDEPENDENCE,
AND TO MARK A MEMORABLE SPOT ON
THE BATTLEFIELD OF MONMOUTH,
THIS TABLET IS PLACED BY MONMOUTH CHAPTER,
DAUGHTERS OF THE AMERICAN REVOLUTION,
SEPTEMBER 26, 1901.

Historic plaque from the Daughters of the American Revolution, commemorating the Battle of Monmouth. Old Tennent Cemetery, Manalapan Township. *Photo by M. Gabriele.*

the location of the tavern "fills in a gap in the topographical understanding of the southern approach to Monmouth."

In the years following the war, Robins Tavern operated as a hotel and became known as the Willow Tree Tavern. "It survived until 1948, when, derelict and frail, it was demolished," Craig writes. On June 5, 1941, the *Asbury Park Press* newspaper reported that the Willow Tree had fallen victim to the ravages of time and weather. Craig, in the notes for his article, wrote that he saw remnants of the tavern's foundation "on many occasions in the late 1960s and early 1970s."

WEDDINGS, FERRIES AND FOX HUNTING

On November 4, 1773, Elizabeth Griscom, a "well-bred young Quaker lady," and John Ross, the son of the assistant rector of Christ Episcopal Church in Philadelphia, boarded a Philadelphia/Gloucester ferry and made their way to Hugg's Tavern in Gloucester Town, where they exchanged wedding vows, having obtained a marriage license from New Jersey governor William Franklin. Historian Louisa W. Llewellyn writes that the couple had eloped and kept their wedding vows secret because of their different faiths.

William Hugg [the son of tavern owner Joseph Hugg] *not only helped* [his friend] *John* [Ross] *plan for the elopement, but also loaned him the money to post the bond required and prepared the wedding feast. A bond of £500 was required by New Jersey law to guarantee that the bride was 21 years old and did not have any disabilities. Since John Ross was just beginning a business as an upholsterer, he did not have this large sum of money. William Hugg came to his rescue. The couple and the patrons of the inn enjoyed a hearty wedding feast prepared by* [the tavern]. *To avoid suspicion, Elizabeth and John returned to Philadelphia before nightfall. However, the story of the elopement became known in the spring of 1774 and angered friends, relatives and the Quaker deacons.*

Ross purchased a house at 239 Arch Street in Philadelphia and taught his wife, Elizabeth, sewing and upholstering skills; she assisted him in the business. In the ensuing years, she came to be known as Betsy Ross, an iconic figure in American history and credited by some historians as the creator of the original thirteen-star American flag.[277] Other historians recognize Francis Hopkinson of Bordentown, a signer of the Declaration of Independence, as the designer of the flag.

The first tavern licenses in Gloucester Town were issued in 1692 to Mary Spey, George Webb and Matthew Medcalfe. Llewellyn writes that Hugg's Tavern became the most famous establishment in Gloucester Town. The county board of freeholders granted Joseph Hugg, the father of William, a license, and he built the tavern in 1720 and 1721. William assumed management of the tavern in 1741 and operated it throughout the Revolutionary War. "The fame of Hugg's food spread among the prominent men of Philadelphia and in 1766 a number of them organized the Fox Hunting Club," and the tavern became the club's primary gathering place. Hugg's became the meeting place for the Gloucester committees of safety, correspondence and observation. Local militias met at the tavern and stored their weapons. County freeholders occasionally held municipal sessions there, and when the Gloucester County buildings were destroyed by fire in 1786, various county meetings were housed at Hugg's Tavern. Despite local efforts to save the historic structure, the building was torn down in 1927.[278]

Members of the Fox Hunting Club also met at Death of the Fox, a tavern in Greenwich Township, Gloucester County. A man named Christopher Taylor built the tavern in 1727 and operated it for seven years. Taylor knew the Hugg family, which provided his connection with the Fox Hunting Club as well as the inspiration for the tavern's unique name. In

Hugg's Tavern, Gloucester. *Courtesy of Bonny Beth Elwell, Camden County Historical Society.*

1774, William Eldridge purchased the tavern, and the following year, he received a license from the Gloucester County Court. Eldridge ran the tavern until 1783.[279]

A public sale notice in Gloucester County, dated March 28, 1774, might have caught the eye of Eldridge.

> *To be sold by public vendue; that old accustomed inn, formerly kept by John Comron, deceased, known by the tavern called the Death of the Fox…containing 198 acres of land and meadow. The land, for the most part, is very good and produceth excellent crops of grain and very good pasture. Thereon is a two-story stone dwelling house with four rooms on a floor, kitchen and other out-houses, a pump of good water, barn and stables, a very good apple orchard, an excellent garden with a considerable quantity of currant bushes, off of which may be made several barrels of wine yearly.*

The 1774 auction sales notice made mention of a tributary of the Delaware River, describing it as "a good navigable creek, which makes it very convenient in getting spirits, wine, beer, oats or any other necessary from Philadelphia on the shortest notice and at a very small expense."

Today, the old tavern is privately owned in Clarksboro, near the intersection of Routes 551 and 678, and a short distance from Manuta

Death of the Fox Tavern, Clarksboro. *Courtesy of Jim and Nancy Sery.*

Creek. Jim and Nancy Sery purchased the property as their residence in 1994 and have done careful restoration work and research over the years, including the removal of two layers of stucco to expose the structure's colorful fieldstone exterior. Jim, in a November 2021 interview, said the home's interior has eight rooms and seven fireplaces. According to his research, the tavern, described as a "common ale house," served as a recruiting station for local militias and became a comfortable place for merchants and farmers to meet and conduct business.

William Royden was one of the first Delaware River ferry boat operators. He received his license on January 1, 1688, issued by the general court then sitting in Gloucester. This license provided that the ferry was to start from a point between Newton and Cooper creeks (in Camden). "Royden was permitted to charge six pence for every person he conveyed across the river and twelve pence for every man and horse. He also was a land owner and a licensed tavern keeper, and his public house stood near the foot of Cooper Street, Camden. In 1689 he sold his ferry to William Cooper."[280]

FATHER AND SON

On May 7, 1783, the *New Jersey Gazette* reported that the

> *gentlemen in the vicinity of the fourth regiment of the Hunterdon militia…* [had] *fixed on this day* [April 28, 1783] *to celebrate that on which the peace* [of the Revolutionary War] *was so happily concluded. The regiment, being paraded by and under the command of Colonel* [John] *Taylor, at twelve o'clock at the flag staff, his excellency, the governor's proclamation was read, which was afterward announced by a discharge of thirteen rounds, each consisting of a platoon of infantry, accompanied with the cheerful huzzahs of a respectable number of spectators, who were assembled on this joyous occasion.*

After a short address by the Reverend Doctor John Rodgers, the company "retired thither to enjoy entertainment provided at the Whitehouse Tavern [in Readington], where thirteen toasts were drank." The party lasted until six o'clock, when the company rested, "having spent the day with that festivity, decency and good order that became a virtuous and free people." The thirteen toasts, anticipating the Treaty of Paris, praised the people of America: "May they ever be independent of and in friendship with all the world; Generals Washington and [Nathanael] Greene; the American delegation, which negotiated the Paris treaty; Mrs. Washington and the Whig ladies of America; and the memory of all who have lost their lives in defense of our liberties."[281]

By contrast, just six years earlier, it was a far less jubilant scene at the Whitehouse Tavern, with the Continental army still locked in the throes of war. A letter sent by George Washington, dated July 25, 1777, from his Pompton Plains headquarters (today's Schuyler Colfax House in Wayne), ordered baker Christopher Ludwick to produce a large amount of bread for the hungry troops (mentioned in "Our Daily Bread" in chapter 2). Washington, who was in Pittstown (fifteen miles west of Readington), wrote to Ludwick:

> *You will therefore immediately upon the receipt of this send all* [bread] *that is ready down to Coryells Ferry* [in Lambertville], *except about two thousand weight, which is to be sent to the place called the Whitehouse* [tavern], *and there wait for the division of the Army, which is with me. I expect to be in that neighborhood the night after tomorrow, if the*

weather is fair. You will continue baking as fast as you can because two other divisions will pass through Pittstown and will want bread. You are to hire wagons to transport the bread, and if they cannot be easily hired, they must be pressed.[282]

Historian Stephanie B. Stevens said the village of Whitehouse took its name from the Whitehouse Tavern, operated by Revolutionary War soldier Abraham Van Horne and so named because of its white-painted exterior. Interviewed in July 2020 at the Daughters of the American Revolution Old Whitehouse Chapter's historic memorial cemetery, Stevens said the tavern was located just off today's Route 22, diagonally across from the cemetery and near the Rockaway Creek. Van Horne's grave is located in the cemetery with a plaque that reads: "Host to General Washington at the Old Whitehouse."[283]

Van Horne's father, also named Abraham Van Horne and also buried in the historic cemetery, purchased land in the district in 1729 and around 1750 built his tavern and a gristmill "a short distance upstream from the confluence of the two Rockaway [creek] branches." His son Abraham assumed responsibility for managing the tavern following his father's

Memorial plaques for Abraham Van Horne and Abraham Van Horne, father and son. Daughters of the American Revolution Memorial Park, Readington Township. *Photo by M. Gabriele.*

death.[284] On October 19, 1898, the *Hunterdon County Republican* reported that "the oldest house and landmark in Whitehouse, [the tavern] is a complete wreck. The structure tumbled down Wednesday [October 12] and is now a heap of bricks."

Meeting with the Sons of Liberty

Francis McShane, the town clerk of Bethlehem, Hunterdon County, transcribed minutes of a town meeting held at the home of David Reynolds on March 11, 1766, responding to a request made by the Sons of Liberty of Lower Hunterdon County. "It was agreed and concluded that…a number not exceeding three men should be chosen in this township, who should have full power to represent the inhabitants thereof, and meet their brethren at the house [tavern] of John Ringoes." The Bethlehem gathering selected Abraham Bonnell, John Rockhill and David Reynolds (believed to be the same David Reynolds mentioned earlier, the proprietor of Van Syckel Tavern) to meet with the Sons of Liberty at Ringoes' Tavern "and perform every act and thing that will redound to the honor of the town and for the benefit of the province in general. And whereas it is absolutely necessary that the operation of all unconstitutional acts should be opposed, and in particular that worst of all acts called the Stamp Act."[285] One member of the trio, Abraham Bonnell, would go on to join the Second Hunterdon County Militia Regiment and establish his own tavern in Clinton, known then as Hunt's Mills (see the following section, "Bonnell's Tavern").

The proposed meeting at Ringo's Tavern (sources use this spelling as well as "Ringoes" for the name of the tavern and town) reflected the early stirrings of colonial rebellion. The Stamp Act, passed by the British Parliament on March 22, 1765 (and repealed the following year), would have imposed a direct tax on all documents in the American colonies.[286] Funds raised by the tax would have helped Britain replenish finances from the Seven Years' War with France. It would have imposed a direct tax on the colonists and required that all legal documents and printed materials have "a tax stamp provided by commissioned distributors, who would collect the tax in exchange for the stamp. The law applied to wills, deeds, newspapers, pamphlets, playing cards and dice."[287]

Documents from the Flemington-based Hunterdon County Historical Society contained Ringo family information, including a family history researched and written by David Leer Ringo. One ancestor, Jan (John)

Artist's drawing of Ringo's Tavern. *Courtesy of the Hunterdon County Historical Society.*

Philipszen Ringo, was a sailor who landed in a port in Spain around the year 1684. There, he was abducted and taken prisoner on a pirate ship. He escaped and sailed to North Carolina and then New York. "Tradition has it that he decided to settle far back in the wilds of New Jersey. Early tales of New Jersey say that when surveyors for the West Jersey Proprietors first came through this part of the country to lay out tracts, they found a John Ringo, living in a log cabin at the crossing of Indian trails near New Hope, Pennsylvania." The surveyors accepted Ringo's kind offer of food, shelter and drink. Apparently, these surveyors told friends and associates of this unexpected hospitality experience, and other travelers began to arrive at Ringo's cabin, which sparked the tradition of family taverns. John Ringo died around 1725.

During the 1720s, members of the Ringo family purchased land in Hunterdon County (some of which is now part of Mercer County). In 1730, Philip Ringo (a grandnephew of the aforementioned John Ringo) sold a mill in Hopewell and became the owner of a tavern in Amwell Township. Theophilis Ketchum purchased a twenty-five-acre tract of land in Amwell Township in 1726 and opened a tavern; however, he died just three years later. It's not clear whether John Ringo purchased and reopened Ketchum's existing tavern or built his own new tavern. "It was not until August 6, 1736

Historic marker, Ringo's Tavern, East Amwell Township. *Photo by M. Gabriele.*

that Philip Ringo received a deed for a five-acre plot of land at the crossroads in Amwell Township [today the center of Ringoes]. The indenture referred to Philip Ringo as an 'inn holder.'" By the 1760s, Philip's son, John, had taken over the tavern business.[288]

Fire destroyed the tavern on April 18, 1840.[289] Another dwelling was built and today stands on the same site as the tavern.

REBUILDING A FAMILY LEGACY

Hank Bonnell spends many a day rebuilding his family's historic tavern, located on Pittstown Road in Clinton. His eighth-great-grandfather, Abraham Bonnell (1732–1797), who served as a lieutenant colonel for the Second Hunterdon County Militia Regiment, opened the tavern in 1767. The lieutenant colonel's father, also named Abraham Bonnell, purchased the "old tavern lot" for his son. Stagecoaches used the tavern as a stop on an old colonial route that stretched from Easton, Pennsylvania, passed through Hunt's Mill (today's Clinton) and terminated near Perth Amboy. It had a stable for stage horses, and "there was a bar where apple and corn whiskey was sold to thirsty wayfarers."[290]

Interviewed in February 2022, Hank Bonnell is dedicated to restoring and researching the old tavern and has the original deed, inscribed on sheepskin, dated May 1, 1767. He also has documents that show a copy of the tavern's original license, dated May 2, 1768. Based on his research, Hank Bonnell believes that an existing structure stood on the property, which his ancestor converted into Bonnell's Tavern.

Bonnell's Tavern became a gathering spot for local Patriots. A document from the archives of the Hunterdon County Historical Society states:

> *In the latter part of 1775, Charles Stewart* [who became the "Commissary General of Issue" for the Continental army], *on his return from a session of the Provincial Congress of New Jersey, where he had gone as a delegate, called a meeting of the inhabitants of this part of the county at Bonnell's Tavern and a regiment of "minute men" was organized. This was the regiment, which was ordered by the Provincial Congress on February 15, 1776, to march under the command of Charles Stewart. In the following year, Abraham Bonnell was elected lieutenant colonel of the Second Regiment of the Hunterdon County militia. In civil affairs he* [Bonnell] *evinced a keen interest and was a member of the township committee and the board of freeholders.*

Prior to operating Bonnell's Tavern, either Abraham Bonnell or Lieutenant Colonel Abraham Bonnell briefly became involved in a separate tavern: the Boar's Head, located in Croton, ten miles south of Clinton. Marfy Goodspeed, an author and historian associated with the Hunterdon County Historical Society, writes that she uncovered a 1762 tavern license application from Daniel Pegg that named Abraham Bonnell as the tavern keeper. "I doubt that Abraham Bonnell stayed long at the Boar's Head,"

Bonnell's Tavern, Clinton (under construction). *Photo by M. Gabriele.*

Goodspeed states. "In the 1760s [he] bought a tract of land near Clinton, where the landmark Bonnell's Tavern was established."[291]

A newspaper article cited the Boar's Head Tavern in a notice of a property sale to be held on April 19, 1758: a public vendue for a certain tract of land in the Great Swamp in Amwell, in the County of Hunterdon.[292] The existence of the Boar's Head and Abraham Bonnell's involvement in it provides the background on the inspiration and experience he needed to establish Bonnell's Tavern.

"AROUSE, MY COUNTRYMEN!"

The handwriting, quite literally, was on the wall at Matthew Potter's tavern in Bridgeton in 1775 and 1776, as revolutionary ferment simmered in Cumberland County. There were several taverns in Bridgeton (known as Cohansey Bridge until 1765) during this period, but Potter's establishment attracted a group of writers and Patriot intellectuals that included Joseph Bloomfield and Richard Howell, both of whom would go on to serve as New Jersey governors.[293]

The Patriot authors posted a handwritten public notice, the *Plain Dealer*, inside Potter's Tavern on December 21, 1775—a preview describing how they would speak out on issues of the day in a series of political essays. "As the circumstances of the times loudly call for every individual for the good of his country and fellow creatures…that the most important service that they can render to society will be to communicate, weekly, to their neighbors the result of their enquiries and speculations on political occurrences and other important subjects particularly calculated to suit this place."

Eight editions of the *Plain Dealer* were hung on the wall of Potter's Tavern from December 25, 1775, to February 12, 1776. The most forthright essay appeared in the February 5, 1776 edition:

> *Must not every son of liberty, both here and in Great Britain, abhor and despise that stubborn and hard-hearted Pharaoh* [King George III], *who disgraces a crown he was never worthy of by giving sanction to such acts of injustice and barbarity. Arouse my Countrymen! Let us draw our swords and never return them into their scabbards till we have rescued our country from the iron hand of tyranny, and secured the pure enjoyment of liberty to generations to come.*[294]

The *Plain Dealer*, no. 3, January 8, 1776. *Photo courtesy of Tara Maharjan, processing archivist, Alexander Library's Special Collections and University Archives, Rutgers University.*

Bob Francois, interviewed in September 2022, who has served as curator of the tavern property with the Cumberland County Historical Society for forty years, said the original Cumberland County Courthouse, erected in 1752, was adjacent to Potter's Tavern. Lawyers, judges and government leaders frequented the establishment and would have seen the *Plain Dealer*

Potter's Tavern, Bridgeton. *Photo courtesy of Brittney Ingersoll, curator, Cumberland County Historical Society, Greenwich.*

notices. The tavern's first floor included two taprooms, a kitchen and a separate, private meeting room used by courthouse officials, according to Francois. "This wasn't a poor-man's tavern."

The tavern's history dates back to a blacksmith named John Hall, who kept a tavern at his home in the 1750s. Fire destroyed his dwelling, but Hall rebuilt and obtained another tavern license in December 1759. Joseph Bishop, around 1765, followed Hall as a proprietor. Captain Charles Clunn owned the tavern building and rented it to Matthew Potter. Potter, born in Ulster, Ireland, in 1734, came to Connecticut in 1740 and later moved to Philadelphia. He relocated to Bridgeton in the 1770s and set up a blacksmithing business while running the tavern, located on the north side of Broad Street. The tavern closed around 1788, and Potter died in 1808. The building sat abandoned for many years, until Bridgeton acquired the property in 1958. The site was placed on the state and national registers of historic places and today is owned by Cumberland County and operated by the county historical society.[295]

MORRISTOWN

During the Continental army's 1777 winter encampment (January through May), Colonel Jacob Arnold hosted Washington and his staff at his tavern in Morristown, which served as Washington's headquarters. The general and his troops marched into Morristown following the Battle of Princeton in early January that year.[296] Arnold, the captain of a light-horse cavalry in the Morris County militia, served as a gracious "mine host" to Washington. The establishment previously had been known as Kinney's Tavern, as Arnold had a partnership with Thomas Kinney, the high sheriff of Morris County, who owned the tavern. Kinney turned over the tavern to Arnold.[297]

Historian Philip H. Hoffman writes that the tavern was situated on the north side of the Morristown Green. "There was a large farm attached to the Arnold Tavern, running back to the Jockey Hollow Road and across to Bridge Street, now Speedwell Avenue. [Colonel Arnold] was an ardent Patriot and his horsemen were filled with the same spirit. His tavern became the rallying point and headquarters for many patriotic and loyal American citizens and

Arnold Tavern, Morristown. Drawing by Suzy Howell, 1891. *Courtesy of the Morristown and Morris Township Library.*

officials of the surrounding country before and up to the time Washington sought its shelter and made it his headquarters during the disheartening and severe winter of 1777." It's believed that Arnold's father, Samuel Arnold, erected the tavern—a three-story structure—sometime between 1735 and 1750. The tavern ballroom held Morristown social events, such as assembly balls for officers, along with meetings of the local Masonic lodge.[298]

Historic marker, Arnold Tavern, Morristown. *Photo by M. Gabriele.*

On March 1, 1777, Alexander Hamilton joined Washington as an aide-de-camp (a military administrative assistant). Hamilton moved into the tavern headquarters and "began drafting letters and handling correspondence for Washington." The general and his troops left Arnold Tavern on May 28, 1777, to begin the summer military campaign.[299] Hamilton met his future wife, Elizabeth Schuyler, the daughter of General Philip Schuyler, during this winter encampment.

Arnold Tavern passed through the hands of many owners until 1886, when it faced demolition. Julia Keese Nelson Colles, a founding member of the Women's Board of the New Jersey Historical Society and a member of the Daughters of the American Revolution, determined to save the building and arranged to move it to her family's estate on Mount Kemble Avenue, until it was purchased by the All Souls Hospital Association.[300] Restored and expanded, the old tavern structure became part of the hospital complex in 1892. In the early morning hours of April 4, 1918, a fire destroyed the hospital and the remnants of Washington's historic headquarters. The three-column headline on page 1 of a Morristown newspaper, from the archives of the Morristown and Morris Township Library, reads: "Forty Patients Rescued from All Souls Hospital Early This Morning When Upper Floors Burn; Volunteers Carry Out Sufferers While Roof Is Mass of Flames."

The Continental army's second encampment in Morristown began when troops arrived in December 1779. They dug in at the Jockey Hollow forest and prepared for another brutal winter season. George and Martha Washington and their entourage were welcomed at the mansion of Colonel Jacob Ford Jr., which became Washington's headquarters for this

Pictured is a recreated military aide's room at Ford Mansion, Washington's Headquarters, Morristown. *Photo by M. Gabriele.*

encampment.[301] Today, the mansion is part of Washington's Headquarters, Morristown National Historical Park.

Dickerson's Tavern (also known as Norris's Tavern) housed drama in Morristown during this second encampment. The tavern became the courtroom for the trial of Major General Benedict Arnold.[302] Arnold, during his command in Philadelphia in June 1778, "formed a very suspicious partnership, by which goods not wanted for the public use were purchased with public funds and sold for the benefit of himself and partners." According to the trial transcripts (Headquarters, Morristown, December 22, 1779), "The general court martial [of Arnold], whereof Major General Howe is president, [is] to sit tomorrow morning, ten o'clock at Norris' Tavern." The trial, led by Major General Robert Howe, concluded on January 26, 1780, with Arnold being acquitted of two of the four charges against him.[303]

Benedict Arnold's more serious crime, which forever branded him as a traitor, occurred on September 21, 1780. Given command of West Point, New York, Arnold secretly contacted a British army officer in a plot to hand over control of the fort in exchange for money. After the conspiracy was uncovered, Arnold fled and joined the British army. He moved to England and died in London on June 14, 1801.[304]

The Dickerson tavern. (a) Spring M. - Water 1775.

Dickerson's Tavern, Morristown. *Courtesy of the Morristown and Morris Township Library.*

A newspaper clipping from the archives of the Morristown and Morris Township Library includes an ad from the October 25, 1773 edition of the *New York Gazette*: "Captain Peter Dickerson acquaints the pubic that he has now opened a tavern in the house lately occupied by Samuel Haynes in Morristown, New Jersey, where travelers and others will meet good entertainment and the best of liquors, always kept for the benefit of the pubic." A year later, the same newspaper published an ad that provided an account of the stage wagons running at Dickerson's Tavern. In 1779, Dickerson leased the tavern to Robert Norris, and it became known as Norris's Tavern during the trial of Benedict Arnold.[305]

Dickerson, a loyal Patriot, was politically active and in 1775 served as a member of the First Provincial Congress of New Jersey and commanded the Fifth Company, Third Battalion. "On January 10, 1776, the Continental Congress called for another battalion from New Jersey. And in accordance with the recommendation of the Provincial Congress this command was organized at once. Of one of the companies of this battalion, Peter Dickerson of Morristown, was the captain."[306]

The Alliance, Morristown Green, depicts (*left to right*) the Marquis de Lafayette, Alexander Hamilton and George Washington. *Photo by M. Gabriele.*

Another newspaper article from the Morristown and Morris Township Library's archives, dated June 11, 1936, reported that Dickerson's Tavern "is one of the few buildings of the colonial period, which remains standing in its original position in Morristown [at the corner of Spring and Water Streets]." Morristown embarked on a far-reaching urban renovation program that began in the late 1960s and lasted into the mid-1980s. The *New York Times* reported that "for many years, it seemed that the urban-renewal project would turn out to be anything but a success. The old buildings on the [Headquarters Plaza] site were razed or, in the case of two historic structures, moved in 1968." The story didn't identify the "two historic structures."[307] It's believed that Dickerson's Tavern most likely was demolished in 1971 during the urban renewal project.

Today, Morristown's grand Revolutionary War legacy is documented through historic plaques, statues and monuments found on buildings and streets surrounding the city's beloved Green. The two-and-a-half-acre Green underwent a $1 million beautification project, highlighted by the unveiling on October 10, 2007, of three life-size statues—created by Studio EIS of Brooklyn—called *The Alliance*. The statues depict George Washington, Alexander Hamilton and the Marquis de Lafayette and commemorates the meeting on May 10, 1780, between Lafayette and Washington during the second Morristown encampment.[308]

"A HEART FULL OF LOVE AND GRATITUDE"

The second Morristown encampment ended in June 1780. The war effort culminated with the surrender by the British at Yorktown, Virginia, on October 19, 1781, the signing of the Treaty of Paris on September 3, 1783, and the ratification of the treaty by the Continental Congress on January 14, 1784.[309]

On Thursday, December 4, 1783, George Washington bid farewell to his top military officers during an emotional ceremony at Fraunces Tavern in Lower Manhattan. Washington, having filled a glass of wine, addressed his brave fellow soldiers.[310]

Left: Historic plaque, Fraunces Tavern, New York City. *Photo by M. Gabriele.*

Below: Fraunces Tavern, New York City. *Photo by M. Gabriele.*

With a heart full of love and gratitude, I now take leave of you. I most devoutly wish that your latter days may be as prosperous and happy as your former ones have been glorious and honorable.

Following this toast, at around two o'clock in the afternoon, Washington and his generals left the tavern, passed through a corps of light infantry and walked to Whitehall Wharf, where they boarded a barge and crossed the Hudson River, landing at "Powles Hook" (Paulus Hook, Jersey City). From there, Washington traveled to Annapolis, Maryland, and formally resigned his commission as commander in chief to the Continental Congress on December 23, 1783.[311]

THE CROSSROADS OF THE REVOLUTION, THE FOOTPRINTS OF OUR FOREBEARERS

ħistory is serious business. We must rely on old archives. We must stick to the facts. But history is not just a checklist of the facts; it's really storytelling. To make our historical accounts interesting and readable, we must tell a story. Each generation tells and re-tells the story to make it comprehensible and understandable. As scholars we want the facts, but as human beings we also understand things through our emotions and feelings."

So said Angus Kress Gillespie, PhD, in an October 2021 interview. Gillespie is a professor of American studies at Rutgers University and an author, folklorist and founder of the New Jersey Folk Festival. In Gillespie's book *Looking for America on the New Jersey Turnpike* (written with Michael Aaron Rockland), he writes about facts regarding the construction of the turnpike, but he also captures the feeling of awe at its size and its round-the-clock heavy flow of traffic. In his book *Twin Towers: The Life of New York City's World Trade Center*, he details the facts of its architectural design and construction but also documents feelings of horror and anger after the terrorist attack of September 11. "Emotions are part of the story."

It's an act of stewardship when stories are handed down generation to generation, linking past and present. The language of history creates a sense of place for individuals and communities. Jennifer Dowling Norato, the peer editor for this book and a teacher in the Emerson public school district, faces the daily challenge of connecting her students to the world around them. "The most effective way to do this is to show students how history has affected their lives," she said. "Two hundred and fifty years later,

Angus Kress Gillespie. *Photo by M. Gabriele.*

the American Revolution can and must still be connected to the world around us." Her hope is that students will become stewards of this legacy.

Norato finds inspiration in history-focused organizations like the Alexander Hamilton Awareness Society and the Daughters of the American Revolution. "Even with a master's degree with a concentration in history, I'm always learning something new. Fellow historians look to better understand the world and how it continues to influence our existence. The proverbial thirst for knowledge is what keeps me going. I like to think my excitement and passion is felt by others when I can share this knowledge."

Andrew Shankman, PhD, the editor of the *Journal of the Early Republic* and a professor of history and the graduate program director in the Department of History at Rutgers University–Camden, said many people believe that the Revolutionary War happened because of the long development of a distinct American nationalist consciousness, which made a declaration of independence inevitable. But, he said, that wasn't the case. "American colonies in the early 1700s embraced British culture. They were conscious and proud of their British identity. The idea of a 'revolution' would have run counter to this engagement in British cultural identity."

That engagement began to change by 1763, following the end of the French and Indian War. The British monarchy taxed the colonies to help pay for an expensive conflict. American colonists saw "taxation without representation" as a serious intrusion on their cherished British identity. An authoritarian attempt to impose taxes, dictated by the whims of a faraway king, threatened that liberty. According to a blog post on the National Constitution Center website, the protests "were based on a legal principle that the colonial legislatures only had the power to tax residents who had representatives in those legislatures."[312]

Colonists felt that a "tyrannical" monarchy had fundamentally violated their British identity, which led to the anger that produced the desire for independence, according to Shankman, interviewed in August 2021. As tensions escalated, whispers of rebellion grew louder inside village taverns, and British authorities closely monitored these seditious conversations. When the "shot heard 'round the world" rang out on April 19, 1775, at Lexington and Concord, Massachusetts, between the Minutemen and British soldiers, there was no turning back.

Writing a chapter in the book *The Edinburgh Companion to the History of Democracy: From Pre-history to Future Possibilities*, Shankman outlined the political dynamics in the 1770s and 1780s:

> *By 1775, what many in Britain saw as necessary taxation, many in the colonies viewed as encroachment by an imperial government.* [It] *shattered colonists' illusions about their place in the empire. Thomas Paine, in his 1776 pamphlet,* Common Sense, *summed up what many colonists had already concluded: Britain's "mixed and balanced government" had not prevented the king and his ministers from acting tyrannically. The answer was not simply "independence." Independence from Britain, Paine insisted, required independence from things British, particularly hereditary governance. By 1776, the vast majority of colonists understood with Paine that their new nation must be a republic.*
>
> *It was clear that colonial elites could not start a revolution to overthrow imperial authority without also having their own authority seriously tested. The Revolution introduced the possibility of democracy to America. Though largely unexpected in 1776, by the mid-1780s democracy in America was a visible and likely outcome of revolution. From the 1780s onwards, the general view of democracy switched to a debate about what democracy was and how it would actually work. Discussions explored the limits to a majority's power, the powers and prerogatives of minorities, and the existence of fundamental natural rights that the majority was enjoined from violating.*

Nancy Isenberg, PhD, a 1980 graduate of Rutgers University, author and distinguished professor at Louisiana State University, in the preface of her 2007 book *Fallen Founder: The Life of Aaron Burr*, warns against a romanticized reading of human affairs from long ago. "History is not a bedtime story. It is a comprehensive engagement with often obscure documents and books no longer read—books shelved in old archives, and fragile pamphlets contemporaneous with the subject under study—all of which reflect a world view not ours. We cannot make eighteenth-century men and women 'familiar' by endowing them and their families with the emotions we prefer to universalize; nor should we try to equate their politics with politics we understand." Based on this passage from Isenberg, the key to gaining wisdom from history is being dedicated to a "comprehensive engagement," considering a range of information offered by historians that might challenge long-held assumptions.

COLONIAL TAVERNS WERE THE social network in New Jersey during the seventeenth and eighteenth centuries: strongholds for political activities, beacons for travelers and venues for entertainment, merriment, romance, treachery, conversation, reading, debate and libations. The stories from New Jersey's colonial taverns reflect the local history from this era of political and social upheaval, with portraits of "ordinary" lives that were far from ordinary. Taverns played a significant role as the stage for the unfolding drama of a colony transitioning into statehood and making decisions about declaring a war of independence. Taverns were the places where the voices of history took shape in colonial New Jersey. If we listen carefully, those voices still echo today.

Each day in the Garden State, we literally walk along the Crossroads of the Revolution in the footprints of our forebearers—a legacy that lies just below the surface of our everyday lives. The ghosts that linger on these byways sustain our state's collective heritage. Individual sketches of people, places and events presented in this book are illuminating, but when assembled as a whole from numerous sources, a more complete, colorful mosaic emerges—a grassroots saga of New Jersey's Revolutionary spirit and colonial life. This mosaic, this saga is the foundation of our state's living history.

THE *NEW-JERSEY GAZETTE* REPORTED that the village of Princeton and the College of New Jersey (today's Princeton University) hosted jubilant festivities on April 19, 1783, to mark the end of the

Opposite, top: Historic marker, Battle of Monmouth. *Opposite, bottom*: Historic marker, Retreat Route, Englewood.

This page, above left: Historic marker, Quaker Road, Princeton. *This page, above right*: Historic marker, Bethlehem Presbyterian Church, Pittstown, Hunterdon County. *This page, left*: Historic marker, Washington/ Rochambeau National Historic Trail, Route 202, Wayne. *Photos by M. Gabriele.*

war.[313] "When word that peace had been achieved reached New Jersey in early April 1783, Governor William Livingston issued a proclamation heralding the joyous news. Communities throughout the state held public celebrations. The war was over. Jerseymen had peace at last."

Festivities began at one o'clock in the afternoon, with large crowds gathering at College Hall. The taverns of Jacob Hyer and Christopher Beekman provided "entertainments" and hosted guests throughout the day. After the supper hour, dignitaries raised their glasses and gave thirteen toasts throughout the village, accompanied by the discharge of cannons. Among the thirteen toasts, three were especially compelling:

> *To the United States of America; may virtue, patriotism and public honor—the sure basis of free governments—ever be the cement and support of the American union.*
>
> *To an increase of arts, agriculture,* [manufacturing] *and commerce in America, and may republican virtue and frugality take the place of monarchical luxury and extravagance.*
>
> *To the state of New Jersey; may her rulers always possess that wisdom and preserve that dignity, public spirit and integrity necessary to govern so patriotic a republic.*

Avenue of Flags, Clifton City Hall, July 4, 2022. *Photo by M. Gabriele.*

The *New-Jersey Gazette* observed that "houses in the town were splendidly illuminated." The Princeton infantry fired thirteen volleys at eight o'clock in the evening, "with regularity and exactness, after which the company retired, having spent the day with that festivity, decency and good order, which we hope will ever characterize a free and virtuous people."

Here's one more toast: one thousand huzzahs to celebrate "free and virtuous people" everywhere as we approach the 250th anniversary of the Declaration of Independence.

NOTES

Epigraph

1. James Boswell, *The Life of Samuel Johnson, LL.D.*, vol. 2 (London, 1791), 28.

Introduction

2. *Acts of the General Assembly of the State of New Jersey* [August 27, 1776–October 11, 1777] (Burlington, NJ: Isaac Collins, 1778), 92–93.
3. "Constitution of New Jersey; 1776," Lillian Goldman Law Library, https://avalon.law.yale.edu/18th_century/nj15.asp, verified from "Acts of the General Assembly of New Jersey [Burlington, NJ, July 2, 1776], compiled by Peter Wilson, Trenton, 1884," pages 3–10.
4. Samuel Adams Drake, *Old Boston Taverns and Tavern Clubs* (Boston: W.A. Butterfield, 1917), 45–51; Boston Tea Party Ships & Museum, "Sons of Liberty: The Masterminds of the Boston Tea Party," https://www.bostonteapartyship.com/sons-of-liberty.
5. Richard P. McCormick, *New Jersey from Colony to State, 1609–1789* (New Brunswick, NJ: Rutgers University Press, 1964), 86–87.
6. Leonard Lundin, *Cockpit of the Revolution: The War for Independence in New Jersey* (Princeton, NJ: Princeton University Press, 1940), vii, 229, 230.
7. Kieran O'Keefe, "Committees of Safety and the Revolutionary War: Kings District, New York," Emerging Revolutionary War Era, May 20,

2019, https://emergingrevolutionarywar.org/2019/05/20/committees-of-safety-and-the-revolutionary-war-kings-district-new-york/.

8. Edward Mark Lender, "Drinking to Independence, the Revolutionary Role of Taverns in New Jersey," *New Jersey Heritage* 3 (2004): 22–32.

9. Baylen J. Linnekin, "Tavern Talk and the Origins of the Assembly Clause: Tracing the First Amendment's Assembly Clause Back to Its Roots in Colonial Taverns," *Hastings Constitutional Law Quarterly* 39, no. 3 (Spring 2012): 593–628.

10. George Washington, "September. [1787]," Washington Papers, Founders Online, National Archives, https://founders.archives.gov/documents/Washington/01-05-02-0002-0009.

11. "The Constitutional Convention," ConstitutionFacts.com, www.constitutionfacts.com/us-constitution-amendments/the-constitutional-convention.

12. Eric Milzarski, "How George Washington Ran Up a $17,253 Bar Tab 2 Days Before Signing the Constitution," Business Insider, September 5, 2018, https://www.businessinsider.com/george-washington-ran-a-17253-tab-before-signing-the-constitution-2018-9.

Chapter 1

13. Samuel Smith, *The History of the Colony of Nova-Caesaria or New Jersey* (Burlington, NJ, 1765), 175–81.

14. "Records of the Town of Newark," in *Collections of the New Jersey Historical Society*, vol. 6 (Newark, NJ, 1864), 13, 34; Sidney Elizabeth Lyon, *Lyon Memorial, Families of Connecticut and New Jersey* (Detroit, MI: William Graham, 1907), 58.

15. Walter H. Van Hoesen, *Early Taverns and Stagecoach Days in New Jersey* (Associated University Presses, 1976), 15–16.

16. Michael Hewitt, *A Most Remarkable Family, The History of the Lyon Family from 1066 to 2014* (Warrington, England: Author House UK, 2014), 120–25.

17. William Richard Cutter, *Genealogical and Family History of Northern New York* (New York: Lewis Historical Publishing, 1910), 1,138.

18. Charles H. Winfield, *History of the County of Hudson, New Jersey* (New York, 1874), 71, 72, 103, 104.

19. William Nelson, "Some Notes on Matinneconk or Burlington Island," *Pennsylvania Magazine of History and Biography* 10, no. 2 (1886), 214–16.

20. Henry Armitt Brown, *The Settlement of Burlington: An Oration, Delivered in That City, December 6, 1877* […], (Burlington, NJ, 1878), 41–43.

21. Richard Veit and David Orr, *Historical Archaeology of the Delaware Valley, 1600–1850* (Knoxville: University of Tennessee Press, 2014), 52–54.

22. William Nelson, ed., *Patents and Deeds and Other Early Records of New Jersey, 1664–1703* (Baltimore, MD: Genealogical Publishing, 2000), 35.

23. Alice Smith Thompson, *The Drake Family of New Hampshire* (Concord: New Hampshire Historical Society, 1962), 30–32.

24. Descendants of the Founders of New Jersey, www.njfounders.org.

25. Emmet Field Horine, *Daniel Drake (1785–1825), Pioneer Physician of the Midwest* (Philadelphia: University of Pennsylvania Press, 1961), 27–31.

26. John P. Wall, *The Chronicles of New Brunswick, New Jersey, 1667–1931* (New Brunswick, NJ: Thatcher-Anderson, 1931), 9–11.

27. Jeanette K. Muser, *Rocky Hill, Kingston and Griggstown* (Charleston, SC: Arcadia Publishing, 1998).

28. "A Brief History of Kingston," Kingston Historical Society, https://www.khsnj.org/history.html; George Dyson, "The Tavern and the Meeting House," Institute for Advanced Study, Princeton University, 2009, https://www.ias.edu/ideas/2009/george-dyson-tavern-and-meeting-house.

29. "Kingston Mill Historic District," National Register of Historic Places registration form, National Park Service, March 13, 1986.

30. Elizabeth G.C. Menzies, *Millstone Valley* (New Brunswick, NJ: Rutgers University Press, 1969), 42, 44, 46–47.

31. John E. Snyder, *The Story of New Jersey's Civil Boundaries, 1606–1968*, (Trenton: New Jersey Geological Survey, 2004), 9, 13; Joseph R. Klett, *Using the Records of the East and West Jersey Proprietors* (Trenton: New Jersey State Archives, 2014), 1–2, 5–6.

32. John Wall and Harold E. Pickersgill, *History of Middlesex County New Jersey, 1664–1920*, vol. 1 (New York: Lewis Historical Publishing, 1921), 63–64, 233–34, 245.

33. George DeCou, *Burlington: A Provincial Capital* (Philadelphia: Harris and Partridge, 1973), 100–3.

34. John Whiteclay Chambers II, *Cranbury, A New Jersey Town from the Colonial Era to the Present* (New Brunswick, NJ: Rivergate Books, 2012), 7, 8.

35. Albert Henry Smyth, *The Autobiography of Benjamin Franklin* (New York: American Book, 1907), 16; Benjamin Franklin, "Notes on the Journey from Boston to Philadelphia in 1723," Franklin Papers, Founders

Online, National Archives, November 29, 1783, https://founders. archives.gov/documents/Franklin/01-41-02-0161.

36. Steven M. Roth, "Stage Operations and the Mails in New Jersey," New Jersey Postal History Society, May 2013, https://njpostalhistory.org/ may13featuredcover.html.

37. John W. Barber and Henry Howe, *Historical Collections of the State of New Jersey* (New Haven, CT, 1868): 41–42.

38. Frank Woodworth Pine, *The Autobiography of Benjamin Franklin* (New York: Henry Holt, 1916), available online via Project Gutenberg; Alfred M. Heston, *South Jersey, A History, 1664–1924*, vol. 1 (New York: Lewis Historical, 1924), 174.

39. Smyth, *Autobiography of Benjamin Franklin*, 72–75.

40. Al Frazza, "Revolutionary War Sites in Burlington, New Jersey," Revolutionary War New Jersey, https://www.revolutionarywarnewjersey. com/new_jersey_revolutionary_war_sites/towns/burlington_nj_ revolutionary_war_sites.htm.

41. The Encyclopedia of Greater Philadelphia, https:// philadelphiaencyclopedia.org.

42. Smyth, *Autobiography of Benjamin Franklin*, 75–76; Pine, *Autobiography of Benjamin Franklin*.

43. Bartlett Burleigh James and J. Franklin Jameson, *Journal of Jasper Danckaerts, 1679–1680* (New York: Charles Scribner's Sons, 1913), available online via Project Gutenberg.

44. Edwin F. Hatfield, *History of Elizabeth, New Jersey, Including the Early History of Union County* (New York, 1868), 75.

45. James and Jameson, *Journal of Jasper Danckaerts*.

46. Ibid.

47. John Clement, *Sketches of the First Emigrant Settlers in Newton Township, Old Gloucester County, West New Jersey* (Camden, NJ, 1877), 163–66.

Chapter 2

48. Editors of Encyclopaedia Britannica, "Tavern," Britannica, https:// www.britannica.com/topic/tavern.

49. Alice Morse Earle, *Stage-Coach and Tavern Days* (New York: Macmillan, 1900), available online via Project Gutenberg.

50. Charles S. Boyer, *Old Inns and Taverns in West Jersey* (Camden, NJ: Camden County Historical Society, 1962), 4.

51. John T. Cunningham, *New Jersey, America's Main Road* (Garden City, NY: Doubleday, 1966), 283–84.
52. Thomas Fleming, *New Jersey, A History* (New York: W.W. Norton, 1984), 37–39.
53. George DeCou, *Burlington: A Provincial Capital* (Philadelphia: Harris and Partridge, 1973), 96–98.
54. Barber and Howe, *Historical Collections*, 41–42.
55. "Kingston Village Historic District," National Register of Historic Places registration form, National Park Service, November 1989.
56. John W. Barber, *Historical Collections of New Jersey: Past and Present* (published by subscription, 1868).
57. William Nelson, ed., *New Jersey Archives, Colonial Documents, Newspaper Extracts, 1766–1767*, vol. 25 (Paterson, NJ: Call, 1903), 125.
58. John Adams, "John Adams to Abigail Adams, 18 October 1799," Adams Papers, Founders Online, National Archives, https://founders.archives.gov/documents/Adams/04-14-02-0015.
59. KSK Architects Planners Historians, *New Jersey Historic Roadway Study* (New Jersey Department of Transportation, 2011), 110.
60. Charles S. Boyer, *Annals of Camden No. 3—Old Ferries, Camden, New Jersey* (Camden, NJ: County Historical Society, Camden, 1921), 4.
61. Boyer, *Old Inns and Taverns*, 15–16.
62. Lauren Pancurak Yeats, *Linden, New Jersey* (Charleston, SC: Arcadia Publishing, 2002), 29–31.
63. Elmer T. Hutchinson, "The Old Wheat Sheaf Inn," *Proceedings of the New Jersey Historical Society* 5 (1920): 246–48.
64. Kym S. Rice, *Early American Taverns: For the Entertainment of Friends and Strangers* (Chicago: Regnery Gateway, 1983), 73–74.
65. David Steven Cohen, *The Folklore and Folklife of New Jersey* (New Brunswick, NJ: Rutgers University Press, 1984) 94–96.
66. Susan P. Schoelwer, "Tavern Signs Mark Changes in Travel, Innkeeping and Artistic Practice," Connecticut History.org, June 1, 2021, https://connecticuthistory.org/tavern-signs-mark-changes-in-travel-innkeeping-and-artistic-practice/.
67. Marie Murphy Duess, *Colonial Inns and Taverns of Bucks County* (Charleston, SC: The History Press, 2007), 39.
68. Rice, *Early American Taverns*, 79–81.
69. Roth, "Stage Operations."
70. Alison M. Gavin, "'In the King's Service': Hugh Finlay and the Postal System in Colonial America," *Prologue* 41, no. 2 (Summer 2009),

https://www.archives.gov/publications/prologue/2009/summer/finlay.html.

71. Patrick J. Kiger, "How Ben Franklin Established the U.S. Post Office," History.com, August 10, 2020, www.history.com/news/us-post-office-benjamin-franklin.

72. Doug Kiovsky, "The Bordentown Family and the Winds of Dissension," Community News, last updated January 11, 2022, https://www.communitynews.org/towns/bordentown-current/kiovsky-the-bordentown-family-and-the-winds-of-dissension/article_e465dcf7-4d57-5a3d-903b-79143601baa8.html.

73. Major E.M. Woodward and John F. Hageman, *History of Burlington and Mercer Counties, New Jersey* (Philadelphia, 1883), 55, available online via Internet Archive.

74. William Nelson, ed. *Documents Relating to the Colonial History of New Jersey*, vol. 27 (Paterson, NJ: Press Printing and Publishing, 1905), 23.

75. "History," Township of Scotch Plains New Jersey, www.scotchplainsnj.gov/government/history.

76. Cheryl Harned (curator), *A Place of Reading* (online exhibition), 2009, American Antiquarian Society (Worcester, MA), https://www.americanantiquarian.org/Exhibitions/Reading/revolutionary.htm.

77. W.J. Rorabaugh, *The Alcoholic Republic—An American Tradition* (New York: Oxford University Press, 1979), 35.

78. William Nelson, *Some New Jersey Printers and Printing in the Eighteenth Century* (Worcester, MA: American Antiquarian Society, 1911), 3, 16.

79. Richard Edwards, *Industries of New Jersey, Trenton, Princeton, Hightstown, Pennington and Hopewell, Part 1* (New York: Historical Publishing, 1882), 44; Nelson, *Some New Jersey Printers*, 18–19.

80. John R. Anderson, *Shepard Kollock: Editor for Freedom* (Chatham, NJ: Chatham Historical Society, 1975), 1–7; Donald Wallace White, *A Village at War: Chatham New Jersey and the American Revolution* (Rutherford, NJ: Fairleigh Dickinson University Press, 1979), 27–30, 38, 120–22.

81. Nelson, *Colonial History*, vol. 27, 459–60.

82. Ibid., 133.

83. Al Frazza, "Revolutionary War Sites in Shrewsbury, New Jersey," Revolutionary War New Jersey, https://www.revolutionarywarnewjersey.com/new_jersey_revolutionary_war_sites/towns/shrewsbury_nj_revolutionary_war_sites.htm.

84. "Welcome to the Allen House!," Monmouth County Historical Association, www.monmouthhistory.org/tavern-museum-at-the-allen-house.

85. Benjamin Franklin, "The Antediluvians Were All Very Sober," Franklin Papers, Founders Online, National Archives, https://founders.archives.gov/documents/Franklin/01-03-02-0023.

86. Rice, *Early American Taverns*, 94–95.

87. "Rum," George Washington's Mount Vernon, https://www.mountvernon.org/the-estate-gardens/distillery/rum/.

88. Katharine M. Beekman, "A Colonial Capital," *Proceedings of the New Jersey Historical Society* 3 (1918): 25.

89. William Coxe, Esq., *A View of the Cultivation of Fruit Trees and the Management of Orchards and Cider* (Philadelphia, 1817), 92–94.

90. *The Diaries of George Washington*, ed. Donald Jackson, vol. 1, *1748–65* (Charlottesville: University Press of Virginia, 1976), published online by the Library of Congress.

91. John Perritano, "How the Founding Fathers Made Their Beer," *Popular Mechanics*, June 25, 2013, www.popularmechanics.com/home/how-to-plans/how-to/a9066/how-the-founding-fathers-made-their-beer-15627801/.

92. Frank Vriesekoop et. al, "125th Anniversary Review: Bacteria in Brewing: The Good, the Bad and the Ugly," *Journal of the Institute of Brewing* 118, no. 4 (February 12, 2013), https://onlinelibrary.wiley.com/doi/full/10.1002/jib.49.

93. "The Oxford Companion to Beer Definition of Brewing in Colonial America," Craft Beer and Brewing, https://beerandbrewing.com/dictionary/yPV4Boo9uC/.

94. Charles H. Winfield, *Hopoghan Hackingh, Hoboken: Pleasure Resort for Old New York* (New York: Caxton Press, 1895), 8.

95. Robert Feldra, *History of Hudson County, Genealogies of Prominent Families* (Union, NJ: Michel and Rank, 1917), 22.

96. Charles H. Winfield, *History of the County of Hudson, New Jersey* (New York, 1874), 31–32, 43–44.

97. Cornelius Burnham Harvey, *Genealogical History of Hudson and Bergen Counties, New Jersey* (New York: New Jersey Genealogical Publishing, New York, 1900), 17.

98. "[Burlington's] High Street Historic District (boundary increase)," National Register of Historic Places registration form, National Park Service, July 9, 2014.

99. Robert L. Thompson, *Burlington Biographies* (Galloway, NJ: South Jersey Culture and History Center, Stockton University, 2016), 3–4, 9, 38.

100. Thomas Budd, *Good Order Established in Pennsylvania and New Jersey* (Cleveland, OH: Burrows Brothers, 1902; reprinted from the original 1685 edition), 30–36.

101. Arthur D. Pierce, *Smugglers' Woods: Jaunts and Journey's in Colonial and Revolutionary New Jersey* (New Brunswick, NJ: Rutgers University Press, 1992), 179–83; Larry R. Gerlach, *William Franklin: New Jersey's Last Royal Governor* (Trenton: New Jersey Historical Commission, 1975), 31–33.

102. Harry B. Weiss and Grace M. Weiss, *The Early Breweries of New Jersey* (Trenton: New Jersey Agricultural Society, 1963), 14, 33–35.

103. George Washington, "To Make Small Beer," George Washington Papers, Manuscripts and Archives Division, The New York Public Library, https://www.nypl.org/about/divisions/manuscripts-division/george-washington-beer.

104. "Recipe for Small Beer," The Fred W. Smith National Library for the Study of George Washington at Mount Vernon, Virginia, https://www.mountvernon.org/library/digitalhistory/digital-encyclopedia/article/recipe-for-small-beer/.

105. Frank H. Stewart, *Notes on Old Gloucester County, New Jersey*, vol. 1 (Camden, NJ: Sinnickson Chew and Sons, 1917), 293–96.

106. Jeffrey M. Dorwart and Elizabeth A. Lyon, *Elizabeth Haddon Estaugh, 1680–1762* (Haddonfield, NJ: The Historical Society of Haddonfield, 2013).

107. Samuel N. Rhoads, "Haddon Hall of Haddonfield, New Jersey," *Bulletin of Friends' Historical Society of Philadelphia* 3, no. 2 (June 1909): 58–70.

108. "The Revolutionary War Era and Haddonfield's Famous Tavern," Indian King Tavern Museum, www.levins.com/ik7.html.

109. The Women's Project of New Jersey, *Past and Promise: Lives of New Jersey Women* (Syracuse, NY: Syracuse University Press, 1997), 2–3.

110. William H. Benedict, "Early Taverns in New Brunswick," in *Proceedings of the New Jersey Historical Society* 3 (1918), 129–33.

111. "Guide to the Sign of the Unicorn Tavern (Graham's Tavern), Elizabeth, NJ," Records 1765–1794 MG 107, The New Jersey Historical Society, 2004, https://jerseyhistory.org/guide-to-the-sign-of-the-unicorn-tavern-grahams-tavern-elizabeth-njrecords1765-1794mg-107/.

112. Elmer T. Hutchinson, "The Ledger of the Graham Tavern, Elizabethtown, NJ," *Proceedings of the New Jersey Historical Society* 15 (1930): 2–5, via Digital Antiquaria.

113. Stewart, *Notes on Old Gloucester County*, 61–62.

114. Sarah W.R. Ewing and Robert McMullin, *Along Absecon Creek* (Bridgeton, NJ: C.O.W.A.N., 1965).

115. Roth, "Stage Operations," 33.

116. Research at Indian Queen Tavern, Piscataway's East Jersey Olde Town Village, October 21, 2021.

117. John Adams, "Monday September 9, 1776 [from the Autobiography of John Adams]," Adams Papers, Founders Online, National Archives, https://founders.archives.gov/documents/Adams/01-03-02-0016-0187.

118. "The Conference House Museum's Role in Shaping of American History," Conference House, https://theconferencehouse.org/about/history/.

119. "Saving History: Indian Queen Tavern," *Link* (newsletter) 7, no. 3, Raritan Millstone Heritage Alliance (Fall 2006).

120. Charles H. Kaufman, *Music in New Jersey, 1655–1860* (East Brunswick, NJ: Associated University Presses, 1981), 18.

121. Boyer, *Old Inns and Taverns*, 13–14.

122. John Omwake, *The Conestoga Six-Horse Bell Teams of Eastern Pennsylvania* (Cincinnati, OH: Ebbert and Richardson, 1930), 116.

123. Todd Andrlik, "John Dickerson's Hit Single: Liberty Song," Journal of the American Revolution, March 12, 2014, https://allthingsliberty.com/2014/03/the-liberty-song/.

124. John Adams, "Monday August 14 [from the Diary of John Adams]," Adams Papers, Founders Online, National Archives, https://founders.archives.gov/documents/Adams/01-01-02-0013-0001-0005.

125. Jane E. Calvert, ed., "John Dickinson Biography," The John Dickinson Writings Project, https://dickinsonproject.rch.uky.edu/biography.php.

126. Chris Coelho, "Timothy Matlack, Scribe of the Declaration of Independence," Journal of the American Revolution, August 24, 2021, https://allthingsliberty.com/2021/08/timothy-matlack-scribe-of-the-declaration-of-independence.

127. Chris Coelho, "The First Public Reading of the Declaration of Independence, July 4, 1776," Journal of the American Revolution, July 1, 2021, https://allthingsliberty.com/2021/07/the-first-public-reading-of-the-declaration-of-independence-july-4-1776/.

128. "May 19," The Adverts 250 Project, Assumption University, Worcester, Massachusetts, https://adverts250project.org/2018/05/19/may-19-3/.

129. Mary Lynn Ritzenthaler and Catherine Nicholson, "The Declaration of Independence and the Hand of Time," *Prologue* 48, no. 3 (Fall 2016), https://www.archives.gov/publications/prologue/2016/fall/declaration.

130. Joe Pappalardo, "The Science of Saving the Declaration of Independence," *Popular Mechanics*, July 3, 2020, www.popularmechanics.com/technology/a22025447/declaration-of-independence-science/.

131. Dr. Joseph M. Vitolo, "History of Penmanship: The Scribes Who Lettered the Declaration of Independence and the US Constitution," The Washington Calligraphers Guild, www.calligraphersguild.org/Resources/HistoryOfPenmanship/.

132. "Timothy Matlack, c. 1730–1829," University Archives and Records Center, University of Pennsylvania, https://archives.upenn.edu/exhibits/penn-people/biography/timothy-matlack.

133. Al Frazza, "Revolutionary War Sites in Englewood, New Jersey," Revolutionary War New Jersey, www.revolutionarywarnewjersey.com/new_jersey_revolutionary_war_sites/towns/englewood_nj_revolutionary_war_sites.htm.

134. "Six Places That Raised a Liberty Pole," New England Historical Society, https://www.newenglandhistoricalsociety.com/six-places-that-raised-a-liberty-pole/.

135. Adaline W. Sterling, *The Book of Englewood* (Englewood, NJ: Mayor and Council of the City of Englewood, 1922), 17.

136. Ibid., 19.

137. John C. Fitzpatrick, ed., *The Writings of George Washington from the Original Manuscript Sources 1745–1799*, vol. 19 (Washington, D.C.: United States Government Printing Office, 1937), 439–40.

138. *The Western Brewer* (Chicago: H.S. Rich, 1906), 290–91.

139. George Washington, "From George Washington to Christopher Ludwick, 25 July 1777," Washington Papers, Founders Online, National Archives, https://founders.archives.gov/documents/Washington/03-10-02-0404.

140. Henry C. Corbin and Raphael P. Thian, *Legislative History of the General Staff of the Army of the United States from 1775 to 1901* (Washington, D.C.: Government Printing Office, 1901), 253.

141. Christopher Ludwick, "To George Washington from Christopher Ludwick, January 1780," Washington Papers, Founders Online, National Archives, https://founders.archives.gov/documents/Washington/03-24-02-0262.

142. "Christopher Ludwick, 1720–1801, Soldier, Baker, Patriot, Philanthropist," Pennsylvania People, https://pennsylvaniapeople. weebly.com/christopher-ludwick-level-2.html.
143. Melvin H. Buxbaum, "Cyrus Bustill Addresses the Blacks of Philadelphia," *William and Mary Quarterly* 29, no. 1 (January 1972): 99.
144. Ibid., 106.

Chapter 3

145. Mocure Daniel Conway, *The Life of Thomas Paine*, vol. 1 (New York, 1892), chapter 17, available online via Project Gutenberg.
146. Woodward and Hageman, *Burlington and Mercer Counties*, 471.
147. Alfred M. Heston, *South Jersey, A History, 1664–1924*, vol. 1 (New York: Lewis Historical Publishing, 1924), 112.
148. Philip S. Foner, ed., *The Complete Writings of Thomas Paine* (New York: Citadel Press, 1945), xvi.
149. Conway, *Life of Thomas Paine*, vol. 1, chapter 2.
150. "Benjamin Franklin," History, March 22, 2022, https://www.history. com/topics/american-revolution/benjamin-franklin.
151. J. Warner Phipps, "To Benjamin Franklin from J. Warner Phipps, 28 October 1774," Franklin Papers, Founders Online, National Archives, https://founders.archives.gov/documents/Franklin/01-21-02-0182.
152. "Benjamin Franklin Publishes 'An Open Letter to Lord North,'" History, April 5, 1774, www.history.com/this-day-in-history/benjamin-franklin-publishes-an-open-letter-to-lord-north.
153. "Franklin's Turn: Imperial Politics and the Coming of the American Revolution," *Pennsylvania Magazine of History and Biography* 136, no. 2 (April 2012): 127.
154. Conway, *Life of Thomas Paine*, vol. 1, chapter 6.
155. Conway, *Life of Thomas Paine*, vol. 2, chapter 20.
156. "The Ten Crucial Days: The Path to Trenton," American Battlefield Trust, https://www.battlefields.org/learn/articles/ten-crucial-days-path-trenton.
157. David Hackett Fischer, *Washington's Crossing* (New York: Oxford University Press, 2004), 132.

158. "Crossing of the Delaware," The Fred W. Smith National Library for the Study of George Washington at Mount Vernon, Virginia, www.mountvernon.org/library/digitalhistory/digital-encyclopedia/article/crossing-of-the-delaware/.

159. Fischer, *Washington's Crossing*, 217.

160. William M. Welsch, "Christmas Night, 1776: How Did They Cross?," Journal of the American Revolution, December 24, 2020, https://allthingsliberty.com/2020/12/christmas-night-1776-how-did-they-cross/.

161. Jo Ann Tesuro, *Ewing Township* (Charleston, SC: Arcadia Publishing, 2002), 52.

162. Phillip Thomas Tucker, *George Washington's Surprise Attack* (New York: Skyhorse Publishing, New York, 2016).

163. Al Frazza, "Revolutionary War Sites in Nutley, New Jersey," Revolutionary War New Jersey, https://www.revolutionarywarnewjersey.com/new_jersey_revolutionary_war_sites/towns/passaic_nj_revolutionary_war_sites.htm.

164. George Washington, "From George Washington to John Hancock, 23 November 1776," Washington Papers, Founders Online, National Archives, https://founders.archives.gov/documents/Washington/03-07-02-0139.

165. Joseph Atkinson, *The History of Newark, New Jersey* (Newark, NJ, 1878), 92.

166. Frank John Urquhart, *A History of the City of Newark*, vol. 1 (New York: Lewis Historical Publishing Company, 1913), 420–22.

167. U.S. Army Center of Military History, "Washington Takes Command of Continental Army in 1775," U.S. Army, April 15, 2016, https://www.army.mil/article/40819/washington_takes_command_of_continental_army_in_1775.

168. Charles F. Cummings, "Yes, General George Washington Slept Here. Often, in Fact," Knowing Newark: The *Star-Ledger* Columns, May 16, 1996, https://knowingnewark.npl.org/yes-general-george-washington-slept-here-often-in-fact.

169. Rick Schwertfeger, "Savage Civil War in New Jersey During the American Revolution," *Frontier Partisans*, March 5, 2019, https://frontierpartisans.com/15269/savage-civil-war-in-new-jersey-during-the-american-revolution/.

170. Christopher M. Minty, "Seriously, Though, Was the American Revolution a Civil War?," *The Junto* (blog), June 29, 2015, https://earlyamericanists.com/2015/06/29/amrev_civil_war/.

171. Donald E. Sherblom, *Neighbors at War: The Vought Family and the Revolution* (Annandale, NJ: 1759 Vought House, 2011).

172. Donald E. Sherblom, *The Vought Family: Loyalists in the American Revolution* (Annandale, NJ: 1759 Vought House, 2008).

173. *Minutes of the Provisional Congress and the Council of Safety of the State of New Jersey* [June–August 1776] (Trenton, NJ, 1879), 477–78, available online via HathiTrust.

174. Joseph Fagan, *Stories of West Orange* (Charleston, SC: The History Press, 2014), 9–10.

175. William H. Shaw, *History of Essex and Hudson Counties, New Jersey*, vol. 2 (Philadelphia, 1884), 732.

176. William Nelson, *Documents Relating to the Colonial History of the State of New Jersey, Extracts from American Newspapers, Relating to New Jersey*, vol. 20 (Paterson, 1898), 470–71.

177. Graham Russell Hodges and Alan Edward Brown, *Pretends to Be Free: Runaway Slave Advertisements from Colonial and Revolutionary New York and New Jersey* (New York: Garland, 1994), 165.

178. Edward Raymond Turner, "The First Abolition Society in the United States," *Pennsylvania Magazine of History and Biography* 36, no. 2 (1912): 129–42, https://www.jstor.org/stable/20085586.

179. Robert Morton, "The Diary of Robert Morton," *Pennsylvania Magazine of History and Biography* 1, no. 1 (1877): 1–39, https://www.jstor.org/stable/20084252.

180. Amelia Mott Gummere, *The Journal and Essays of John Woolman* (New York: MacMillan, 1922), 20, 163.

181. Ibid., 74.

182. "John Woolman, 1720–1772," Quakers in the World, https://www.quakersintheworld.org/quakers-in-action/62/John-Woolman.

183. Geoffrey Plank, "The First Person in Antislavery Literature: John Woolman, His Clothes and His Journal," *Slavery and Abolition* 30, no. 1 (March 2009).

184. Karl Frederick Geiser, *Redemptioners and Indentured Servants in the Colony and Commonwealth of Pennsylvania* (New Haven, CT: Tuttle, Morehouse and Taylor, 1901), 5–7.

185. William Nelson, *Colonial History*, vol. 20 (Paterson, 1898), 8–9, 145–46.

186. Samuel Allinson, *Acts of the General Assembly of the Province of New Jersey, from the Surrender of the Government to Queen Anne* […] (Burlington, NJ, 1776), 191–92.

187. Graham Russell Hodges, *Root & Branch: African Americans in New York & East Jersey, 1613–1863* (Chapel Hill: University of North Carolina Press, 1999), 89.

188. *A Treaty between the Government of New Jersey and the Indians Inhabiting the Several Parts of Said Province, Held at Crosswicks in the County of Burlington, January 8 and 7, 1756* (Pennsylvania, 1756), available online via the New Jersey State Library.

Chapter 4

189. The Mantua Township Bicentennial Committee, *A Bicentennial Look at Mantua Township* (Paulsboro, NJ: Paulsboro Printers, 1976), 166.

190. Ibid.

191. Edmund Drake Halsey et al., *History of Morris County New Jersey* (New York, 1882), 246.

192. Gabreil Daveis Tavern brochure, Gloucester Township Historic and Scenic Preservation Committee.

193. Wall and Pickersgill, *Middlesex County New Jersey*, 76–77.

194. *Proceedings of the New Jersey Historical Society*, vol. 7 (1922): 107.

195. "Early Cranbury Inns," Cranbury Historical and Preservation Society, https://www.cranburyhistory.org/about-cranbury-nj.

196. John Whiteclay Chambers II, *Cranbury: A New Jersey Town from the Colonial Era to the Present* (New Brunswick, NJ: Rivergate Books, 2012), 20, 53.

197. George Washington, "From George Washington to John Hancock, 5 January, 1777," Washington Papers, Founders Online, National Archives, https://founders.archives.gov/documents/Washington/03-07-02-0411.

198. Valerie Barnes et al., "Bernardsville, NJ Historic Downtown Walking Tour," Historic Preservation Advisory Committee and Friends of Historic Bernardsville, 2017.

199. "John Parker Tavern," National Register of Historic Places inventory/nomination form, National Park Service, December 14, 1978.

200. Frederick Walter, *The Township of Bedminster* (Bedminster, NJ: Bedminster Township Committee, 1964), 23.

201. Philip Otterness, "The 1709 Palatine Migration and the Formation of German Immigrant Identity in London and New York," *Pennsylvania History*, vol. 66 (1999): 8–20.

202. Peter O. Wacker, *The Musconetcong Valley of New Jersey* (New Brunswick, NJ: Rutgers University Press, 1968).

203. Andrew D. Mellick Jr., *The Story of an Old Farm: Or, Life in New Jersey in the Eighteenth Century* (Somerville, NJ: *Unionist-Gazette*, 1889).

204. Walter, *Township of Bedminster*, 83.

205. Sanford H. Cobb, *The Story of the Palatines* (New York, 1897), 59–61, 68.

206. Theodore Frelinghuysen Chambers, *The Early Germans of New Jersey* (Dover, NJ, 1895), 146–47.

207. Minisink Valley Historical Society (Port Jervis, New York), www.minisink.org.

208. James P. Snell, *History of Sussex and Warren Counties, New Jersey* (Philadelphia, 1881), 26.

209. Benjamin Bailey Edsall and Joseph Farrand Tuttle, *The First Sussex Centennary* (Newark, NJ, 1853).

210. Snell, *Sussex and Warren Counties*, 431.

211. Whitfield Gibbs, *One Hundred Years of the Sussex Register and County of Sussex, New Jersey* (Bowie, MD: Heritage Books, 1992), 14.

212. Snell, *Sussex and Warren Counties*, 154, 431–32.

213. George DeCou, *The Historic Rancocas* (Moorestown, NJ: *News Chronicle*, 1949).

214. The Historical Society of Moorestown, https://moorestownhistory.org.

215. Colin Zimmerman, "The Battle of Crosswicks: Prelude to Monmouth," Journal of the American Revolution, August 4, 2022, https://allthingsliberty.com/2022/08/the-battle-of-crosswicks-prelude-to-monmouth/.

216. Alfred M. Heston, *South Jersey, A History*, vol. 1, *1664–1924* (New York: Lewis Historical Publishing, 1924), 105.

217. William Nelson, *Documents Relating to the Colonial History of the State of New Jersey*, vol. 29 (Paterson: Call, 1917), 32–33.

218. "President-Elect George Washington's Journey to the Inauguration," The Fred W. Smith National Library for the Study of George Washington at Mount Vernon, Virginia, https://www.mountvernon.org/george-washington/the-first-president/inauguration.

219. Donald Johnstone Peck, *General Joseph Bloomfield, A Revolutionary Life* (Staunton, VA: American History Press, 2014), 18, 71.

220. Phill Provance, *A Brief History of Woodbridge, New Jersey* (Charleston, SC: The History Press, 2019), 43.

221. "Historic Sites Inventory," Woodbridge Township Historic Preservation Commission, https://woodbridgehistory.com.

222. Joseph W. Dally, *Woodbridge and Vicinity: The Story of a New Jersey Township* (New Brunswick, NJ, 1873), 98–101.

223. Amy E. Breckenridge, *Disappearing Landmarks of Woodbridge* (n.p., 1946; Woodbridge Public Library Americana collection), 4–5.

224. Doug Wilson, "The Elm Tree Tavern of Woodbridge, New Jersey, 1739–1823," 2021, http://dougwilson.com/Family/fcature/elmtreetavern.asp.

225. John Adams, "1774 Aug. 27. Saturday [from the Diary of John Adams]," Adams Papers, Founders Online, National Archives, https://founders.archives.gov/documents/Adams/01-02-02-0004-0005-0015.

226. "Carpenters' Hall, Philadelphia, September 5, 1774–October 6, 1774," Office of the Historian, U.S. Department of State, https://history.state.gov/departmenthistory/buildings/section2.

227. "The Taverns of Old Princeton," *Nassau Literary Magazine* 62, no. 6 (January 1, 1907), https://papersofprinceton.princeton.edu/princetonperiodicals/?a=d&d=NassauLit19070101-01.2.9&dliv=none&e=-------en-20--1--txt-txIN-------.

228. William Nelson, *Documents Relating to the Colonial History of the State of New Jersey*, vol. 24 (Paterson, NJ: Call, 1902), 532–33.

229. "Taverns of Old Princeton."

230. William Nelson, *Documents Relating to the Colonial History of the State of New Jersey*, vol. 28 (Paterson, NJ: Call, 1916), 422–23.

231. Nelson, *Colonial History*, vol. 29 (Paterson, NJ: Call, 1917), 95.

232. Editors of Encyclopaedia Britannica, "Hudibras," Britannica, www.britannica.com/topic/Hudibras-poem-by-Butler.

233. V. Lansing Collins, "Turning Back the Clocks," *Princeton Alumni Weekly* 29, no. 28 (April 26, 1929).

234. Nelson, *Colonial History*, vol. 29, 238, 252.

235. Collins, "Turning Back the Clocks."

236. Holmes Forsyth, "Class Notes," *Princeton Alumni Weekly* 46, no. 4 (October 12, 1945): 10.

237. John Frelinghuysen Hageman, *History of Princeton and Its Institutions* (Philadelphia, 1879), 42–43.

238. V. Lansing Collins, *Princeton Past and Present* (Princeton, NJ: Princeton University Press, 1945), xv–xvii; "180-Year-Old Tavern Nears Destruction," *Local Express* (Princeton, NJ), July 1, 1937.

239. Philander D. Chase, ed., *The Papers of George Washington: Revolutionary War Series*, vol. 4, *April–June 1776* (Charlottesville: University Press of

Virginia, 1991), 363; Joseph Jackson, "Washington in Philadelphia," *Pennsylvania Magazine of History and Biography* 56, no. 2 (1932): 127–29.

240. Dunlap's Pennsylvania Packet, Monday, May 27, 1776, Library of Congress, Washington, D.C.

241. William A. Whitehead, *Contributions to the Early History of Perth Amboy and Adjoining Country* (New York, 1856), 1–5.

242. Ibid., 260–61.

243. Charles A. Shriner, *Paterson, New Jersey* (Paterson, NJ, 1890), 89.

244. William Nelson, *Colonial History*, vol. 29 (Paterson, NJ: Call, 1917), 471, 512; William Nelson and Charles A. Shriner, *History of Paterson and Its Environs (The Silk City)*, vol. 2 (New York: Lewis Historical Publishing, 1920), 65–66.

245. "On This Day in History—July 10, 1778," Revolutionary War and Beyond, www.revolutionary-war-and-beyond.com/george-washington-picnics-at-great-falls.html.

246. Marcia Dente, *Paterson Great Falls, From Local Landmark to National Historical Park* (Charleston, SC: The History Press, 2012), chapter 2.

247. "July 10, 1778."

248. "Dedication of America's 397th National Park," National Park Service press release, November 3, 2011, www.nps.gov/pagr/learn/news/dedication-of-america-s-397th-national-park.htm.

249. Mary J. Atkinson, "The Old Taverns of New Brunswick," *Somerset County Historical Quarterly* 3 (January 1914), 9–11.

250. Peter Kalm, *Travels into North America*, vol. 1, trans. John Reinhold Forster (London, 1772), 1–22, 178–80.

251. Rebecca Yamin, "Local Trade in Pre-Revolutionary New Jersey," *Northeast Historical Archaeology* vol. 22, article 9 (1993): 123–29.

252. Rebecca Yamin, *Rediscovering Raritan Landing* (Ewing Township, NJ: New Jersey Department of Transportation and the Federal Highway Administration, 2011), 99–100, 103–4, 108.

253. Christian M. McBurney, "The Battle of Bennett's Island: The New Jersey Site Rediscovered," Journal of the American Revolution, July 10, 2017, https://allthingsliberty.com/2017/07/battle-bennetts-island-new-jersey-site-rediscovered/.

254. Jessie Kratz, "Dunlap's Declaration of Independence," *Pieces of History* (blog), July 3, 2018, https://prologue.blogs.archives.gov/2018/07/03/dunlaps-declaration-of-independence/.

255. "The Late Colonel Neilson," *Evening Post* (New York), April 1, 1833, available online via Newspapers.com.

256. John P. Wall, "The New Brunswick of Over a Century Ago," in *Proceedings of the New Jersey Historical Society* 7 (1922): 36.

257. Catherine (Kit) Stahler-Miller, "Unveiling of the Colonel John Neilson Statue in New Brunswick: Reflections of a Descendant," August 21, 2017, Jersey Blue Chapter, National Society of the Daughters of the American Revolution, 2017, www.jerseybluedar.org/blog/unveiling-of-the-colonel-john-neilson-statue-in-new-brunswick-nj-reflections-of-a-descendant.

258. Cheryl Makin, "Revolutionary Moment Comes to Life, 241 Years Later," *Courier News and Home News Tribune* (Somerville, NJ), July 10, 2017.

259. "French Arms Tavern, Trenton, November 1—December 24, 1784," Office of the Historian, United States Department of State.

260. "French Arms Tavern," United Colonies and States of America Capitols, www.unitedstatescapitals.org/p/blog-page.html.

261. William J. Backes, "Landmarks, Taverns, Markets and Fairs," in *A History of Trenton, 1679–1929* (Trenton, NJ: Trenton Historical Society), chapter 4.

262. Nelson, *Colonial History*, vol. 20 (Paterson, NJ: Call, 1898), 168; *A History of Trenton, 1679–1929* (Trenton, NJ: Trenton Historical Society).

263. Backes, "Landmarks, Taverns."

264. *The Jerseyman: A Quarterly Magazine of Local History and Genealogy* 9, no. 2 (1903).

265. "Descendants of Levi Hart," https://freepages.rootsweb.com/~cathie/genealogy/chart.html.

266. Megan E. Springate, "Setting a Public Table: Food and Food Service at Colonial and Early American New Jersey Taverns," paper presented at the Council for Northeastern Historical Archaeology Conference, Trenton, October 23, 2005.

267. Al Frazza, "Revolutionary War Sites in Colts Neck, New Jersey," Revolutionary War New Jersey, https://www.revolutionarywarnewjersey.com/new_jersey_revolutionary_war_sites/towns/colts_neck_nj_revolutionary_war_sites.htm; Matthew H. Ward, "Joshua Huddy: The Scourge of New Jersey Loyalists," Journal of the American Revolution, October 8, 2018, https://allthingsliberty.com/2018/10/joshua-huddy-the-scourge-of-new-jersey-loyalists/; Austin Scott, ed., *Revolutionary History of the State of New Jersey*, vol. 5 (Trenton, NJ: State Gazette, 1917), 424.

268. "Authentic Account of the Taking of Captain Huddy," *The Political Magazine and Parliamentary, Naval, Military and Literary Journal* 4 (August 1782): 468.

269. John E. Stillwell, *Historical and Genealogical Miscellany, Early Settlers of New Jersey and their Descendants*, vol. 5 (New York: n.p., 1932), 43–51.

270. "Throckmorton-Lippit-Taylor Burying Ground," Middletown Township NJ, https://www.middletownnj.org/250/Throckmorton-Lippit-Taylor-Burying-Groun.

271. George Washington, "From George Washington to Major General Charles Lee, 30 June 1778," Washington Papers, Founders Online, National Archives, https://founders.archives.gov/documents/Washington/03-15-02-0655.

272. Gary D. Saretzky, *New Jersey in Focus, Buildings in Monmouth: Stories and Styles* (catalog for the exhibit at the Monmouth County Library Headquarters, organized by the Monmouth County Archives, October 2018), 111.

273. Addendum to *The Village Inn* [Robert Newell House], *Englishtown, Monmouth County, New Jersey*, HABS No. NJ-65 (Rahway, NJ: Historic American Buildings Survey, n.d.), https://memory.loc.gov/master/pnp/habshaer/nj/nj0600/nj0612/data/nj0612data.pdf.

274. Saretzky, *New Jersey in Focus*, 109.

275. Robert W. Craig, "In Search of Robins Tavern: A Long-Vanished Landmark on the Road to the Battle of Monmouth," *New Jersey History* 119, no. 1–2 (Spring/Summer 2001), 55–69.

276. John Whiteclay II Chambers, *George Washington in Cranbury, the Road to the Battle of Monmouth*, 2nd ed. (Cranbury, NJ: Cranbury Historical and Preservation Society, 2010), 9–17.

277. Louisa W. Llewellyn, *First Settlement on the Delaware River: A History of Gloucester City, New Jersey*, (Gloucester City, NJ: Gloucester City American Revolution Bicentennial Committee, 1976), 62–63.

278. Ibid., 57.

279. Nelson, *Colonial History*, vol. 29 (Paterson: Call, 1917): 315.

280. Alfred M. Heston, *South Jersey, A History*, vol. 1, 65.

281. *The Jersey Gazette* (Burlington, NJ), May 7, 1783.

282. George Washington, "From George Washington to Christopher Ludwick, 25 July 1777," Washington Papers, Founders Online, National Archives, https://founders.archives.gov/documents/Washington/03-10-02-0404.

283. Al Frazza, "Revolutionary War Sites in Readington Township, New Jersey," Revolutionary War New Jersey, https://www. revolutionarywarnewjersey.com/new_jersey_revolutionary_war_sites/ towns/readington_township_nj_revolutionary_war_sites.htm.

284. "Whitehouse-Mechanicsville Historic District," National Register of Historic Places registration form, National Park Service, January 30, 2015.

285. James P. Snell, *History of Hunterdon and Somerset Counties, New Jersey* (Philadelphia, 1881), 459.

286. Al Frazza, "Revolutionary War Sites in Ringoes, New Jersey," Revolutionary War New Jersey, https://www.revolutionarywarnewjersey. com/new_jersey_revolutionary_war_sites/towns/ringoes_nj_ revolutionary_war_sites.htm.

287. History.com editors, "Stamp Act," July 31, 2019, www.history.com/ topics/american-revolution/stamp-act.

288. David Leer Ringo, "The First Five Generations of the Ringo Family in America," Ringo Family History Series, vol. 2 (Alhambra, CA: Freeborn Family Organization, 1982), document from the archives of the Hunterdon County Historical Society.

289. "Ringoes Historic District," National Register of Historic Places registration form, National Park Service, November 9, 1999.

290. Samuel Harden Stille, "The Old Bonnell Tavern," Historic Guide Posts, *Plainfield* [NJ] *Courier-News*, April 21, 1933.

291. Marfy Goodspeed, "Boars Head Tavern in the 18th Century," *Hunterdon Historical Newsletter* 49, nos. 2–3 , (Spring/Fall 2013), 1162–64, 1167.

292. Nelson, *Colonial History*, vol. 20, 187.

293. F. Alan Palmer, *Matthew Potter, His Tavern, and the Plain Dealer* (Cumberland County Historical Society, 1980), 1–8.

294. William Nelson, *The Plain Dealer* (n.p., 1894), 26.

295. Sharron Morita, *Bridgeton, New Jersey: City on the Cohansey* (Charleston, SC: Arcadia Publishing, 2012); Carl M. Williams, "Ancient Tavern on Broad Street Hill," *Bridgeton* [NJ] *Evening News*, November 27, 1937; Richard F. Hixson, *The Press in Revolutionary New Jersey* (Trenton, NJ: New Jersey Historical Commission, 1975).

296. "Morristown, New Jersey," The Fred W. Smith National Library for the Study of George Washington at Mount Vernon, Virginia, https:// www.mountvernon.org/library/digitalhistory/digital-encyclopedia/ article/morristown-nj.

297. Kat Kurylko, "Morris County Taverns," Morris County Historical Society, December 2020, https://morriscountyhistory.org/morris-county-taverns.

298. Philip H. Hoffman, *History of the Arnold Tavern, Morristown, New Jersey* (Morristown, NJ: Chronicle Press, 1903), 1–14.

299. "Arnold Tavern," The Alexander Hamilton Awareness Society, http://allthingshamilton.com/index.php/aph-home/74-aph-new-jersey/166-arnolds-tavern.

300. Hoffman, *Arnold Tavern*, 3–6.

301. Ibid., 23–26.

302. Al Frazza, "Revolutionary War Sites in Morristown, New Jersey," Revolutionary War New Jersey, www.revolutionarywarnewjersey.com/new_jersey_revolutionary_war_sites/towns/morristown_nj_revolutionary_war_sites.htm.

303. Francis Suydam Hoffman, *Proceedings of a General Court Martial for the Trial of Major General Arnold* (New York, 1865), 1–3, 144–45.

304. "Benedict Arnold Commits Treason," www.history.com/this-day-in-history/benedict-arnold-commits-treason.

305. William S. Stryker, *Documents Relating to the Revolutionary History of the State of New Jersey*, vol. 1 (Trenton, NJ: John L. Murphy, 1901), 123.

306. Andrew M. Sherman, *Historic Morristown New Jersey: The Story of its First Century* (Morristown, NJ: Howard, 1905), 172, 188.

307. "In New Jersey; Morristown Renewal Still Debated," *New York Times*, June 23, 1985.

308. Minhaj Hassan, "Back to the Green, Park Rededication Draws Hundreds to Morristown," *Daily Record* (Parsippany, NJ), October 11, 2007.

309. "Revolutionary War," History.com, https://www.history.com/topics/american-revolution/american-revolution-history; "Proclaiming Peace, January 14, 1784: Ratification of the Treaty of Paris," Maryland State Archives Museum Online, https://msa.maryland.gov/msa/educ/exhibits/treaty/treaty.html.

310. "Goodbye to General Washington," Library of Congress, https://www.loc.gov/item/today-in-history/december-04/; *Rivington's New-York Gazette and Universal Advertiser, December 6, 1783; C. Edwards Lester, Our First Hundred Years: The Life of the Republic of the United States of America (New York, 1877), 421–23.*

311. Joseph Hillman, "Resignation of Military Commission," Fred W. Smith National Library for the Study of George Washington at Mount

Vernon, https://www.mountvernon.org/library/digitalhistory/digital-encyclopedia/article/resignation-of-military-commission/.

Epilogue

312. National Constitution Center staff, "On This Day: No Taxation Without Representation," ConstitutionCenter.org, October 7, 2022, https://constitutioncenter.org/blog/no-taxation-without-representation.

313. Larry R. Gerlach, ed., "Residents of Princeton Celebrate the End of the War [*New-Jersey Gazette*, April 23, 1783]," in *New Jersey in the American Revolution, 1763–1783: A Documentary History* (Trenton, NJ: New Jersey Historical Commission), https://www.njstatelib.org/wp-content/uploads/slic_files/imported/NJ_Information/Digital_Collections/NJInTheAmericanRevolution1763-1783/9.12.pdf.

SOURCES

Adverts 250 Project (Assumption University, Worcester, MA). https://adverts250project.org.

American Battlefield Trust. www.battlefields.org/about/history.

Bordentown Historical Society. https://bordentownhistory.org/.

Burlington County Historical Society. https://burlingtoncountyhistoricalsociety.org/.

Camden County Historical Society. https://cchsnj.org/.

Chatham Historical Society. https://www.chathamnjhistoricalsociety.org/.

Clifton Public Library. https://cliftonpl.org/

Daughters of the American Revolution. https://www.dar.org.

Descendants of Founders of New Jersey. http://www.njfounders.org.

Emerging Revolutionary War Era. https://emergingrevolutionarywar.org.

Encyclopedia Britannica. https://www.britannica.com.

Encyclopedia of Greater Philadelphia. https://philadelphiaencyclopedia.org.

Ford Mansion, Washington's Headquarters. https://www.nps.gov/morr/learn/historyculture/ford-mansion-washington-s-headquarters.htm.

Founders Online, National Archives. https://founders.archives.gov.

Fred W. Smith National Library for the Study of George Washington at Mount Vernon. https://www.mountvernon.org.

Gloucester Township Historic and Scenic Preservation Committee. https://www.facebook.com/glotwphistory.

Google Books. https://books.google.com.

HathiTrust Digital Library. https://catalog.hathitrust.org.

Historical Society of Pennsylvania. https://hsp.org.

History. https://www.history.com.

The History Girl. http://www.thehistorygirl.com.

Hunterdon County Historical Society. https://hunterdonhistory.org/.

Indian King Tavern Museum. https://www.indiankingfriends.org/.

Internet Archive. https://archive.org/web.

John Woolman Memorial. https://woolmanmemorial.org.

Journal of the American Revolution. https://allthingsliberty.com.

JSTOR. https://www.jstor.org.

Laird and Company. https://lairdandcompany.com/.

Library of Congress. https://www.loc.gov.

Lillian Goldman Law Library, Yale Law School. https://library.law.yale.edu/.

The Link. https://www.raritanmillstone.org.

Making of America. https://quod.lib.umich.edu/m/moa/.

Margaret R. Grundy Memorial Library. https://buckslib.org/sp_faq/ margaret-r-grundy-memorial-library/.

Merchants and Drovers Tavern Museum. https://www. merchantsanddrovers.org/.

Morristown and Morris Township Library. https://mmtlibrary.org/.

Museum of Fine Arts, Boston. https://www.mfa.org/.

Museum of the American Revolution (Philadelphia). https://www. amrevmuseum.org/.

National Constitution Center. https://constitutioncenter.org.

National Gallery of Art (Washington, D.C.). https://www.nga.gov/.

National Register of Historic Places. https://www.nps.gov/subjects/ nationalregister/index.htm.

Newark Public Library. https://www.npl.org/main-library/.

New Jersey Archives. https://www.nj.gov/state/archives.

New Jersey Department of Environmental Protection. https://dep.nj.gov/.

New Jersey Historical Commission. https://www.nj.gov/state/historical/.

New Jersey Historical Society. https://jerseyhistory.org.

New Jersey Monthly. https://njmonthly.com.

New Jersey Postal History Society. https://www.njpostalhistory.org.

New Jersey State Archives. https://www.nj.gov/state/archives/index.html.

New Jersey State Library. https://www.njstatelib.org/.

Newspapers.com. https://www.newspapers.com.

New York Public Library. https://www.nypl.org/locations/schwarzman.

New York Times. https://www.nytimes.com.

Nutley Free Public Library. https://nutleypubliclibrary.org/.

Office of the Historian, United States Department of State. https://
    history.state.gov/.
Project Gutenberg. https://www.gutenberg.org.
Revolutionary War and Beyond. https://www.revolutionary-war-and-
    beyond.com.
Revolutionary War Journal. www.revolutionarywarjournal.com.
Revolutionary War New Jersey. https://www.revolutionarywarnewjersey.com/.
Skylands Visitor. https://njskylands.com.
Smithsonian Magazine. https://www.smithsonianmag.com.
Toledo Museum of Art. https://www.toledomuseum.org/.
Trenton Historical Society. https://trentonhistory.org.
University of Utah, J. Willard Marriott Library. https://lib.utah.edu/.
Washington Crossing State Park. https://nj.gov/dep/parksandforests/
    parks/washingtoncrossingstatepark.html.
Wikipedia. https://www.wikipedia.org/.

Interviews

Banta, Linda. Johnsonburg.
Beekman, John. Jersey City Free Public Library.
Berton, Gary. Officer, Thomas Paine National Historical Association, New
    Rochelle, NY, and coordinator of the Institute for *Thomas Paine* Studies
    at Iona College.
Biron, Janis. Mendham Borough Library.
Bonnell, Hank. Bonnell's Tavern.
Brach, John. Gabreil Daveis Tavern.
Bruder, Charles. Executive director of the John Woolman Memorial
    Association, Mount Holly.
Budd, Thomas. Owner and operator, Barnsboro Inn.
Cahill, Kerry. 1759 Vought House group.
Calvert, Jane E., PhD. John Dickinson Writings Project, University of
    Kentucky.
Castorino, Shelly. Regent, Haddonfield Chapter, Daughters of the
    American Revolution.
Cathcart, Shelley. Curator, Museum of Early Trades and Crafts.
Clark, Ann. Treasurer, Absecon Historical Society.
Colombi, Letitia G. Former mayor of the Haddonfield.

Crenshaw, Marie. Head reference librarian, Clarence Dillon Public Library, Bedminster.

Cruthirds, Carolyn. Museum of Fine Arts, Boston.

Cutler, Tim. *Digital Antiquarian* editor and publisher.

Davis, Paul A. Research assistant, Historical Society of Princeton.

Deal, Nancy Ceperley. Historian, Washington Crossing State Park.

DeFillo, Carlotta. Archival assistant, Staten Island Historical Society, New York.

DePow, Kathleen. Director, Perth Amboy Ferry Slip Museum.

Dorman, Dana. Archivist, Historical Society of Haddonfield.

Dorwart, Jeffery M. Author.

Dyke, John Kerry. Perth Amboy historian.

Elwell, Bonny Beth. Library director, Camden County Historical Society.

Epstein, Rick. Frenchtown historian.

Fagan, Joseph. West Orange historian and author.

Fox, Ed. City planner, historian and consultant.

Francois, Bob. Cumberland County Historical Society.

Gillespie, Angus. Professor of American Studies, Rutgers University.

Hefferan, Amanda. Morris County Heritage Commission.

Henderek, Wayne. Washington Crossing State Park, Titusville.

Hess, Linda, and Michelle Hughes. Historic interpreters at Haddonfield's Indian King Tavern.

Honachefsky, William, Jr. Author and vice president of the Union Forge Heritage Association.

Ingersoll, Brittney. Cumberland County Historical Society.

Johns, Barb. President of the Mount Holly Historical Society, Mount Holly.

Kelley, Karen. Cranbury Historical Society.

King, Judith Wilson. Florence Historical Society.

Kiovsky, Doug. Bordentown Historical Society.

Kordys, Mary Ann, and Eileen Stokes. Washington Township Historical Society, Long Valley.

Laird Dunn, Lisa. Laird and Company.

LaVo, Carl. Author.

Lewis, James. Morristown and Morris Township Library.

Linnekin, Baylen J. The Reason Foundation.

Luck, George, Jr. Kingston Historical Society.

Macechak, Jeff. Burlington County Historical Society.

Maharjan, Tara. Special Collections and University Archives, Archibald S. Alexander Library, Rutgers University.

Maresca, Vincent. Historic preservation specialist in the Historic Preservation Office, New Jersey Department of Environmental Protection.

Martin, Douglas D. Historian, Van Syckel Tavern.

McCarthy, Lynn. Winterthur Museum, Garden and Library.

Mercer, Deborah. New Jersey State Library.

Minty, Christopher F., PhD. Managing editor of the John Dickinson Writings Project at the Center for Digital Editing at the University of Virginia.

Mosley, Joyce Marqurite. Author, historian, Cyrus Bustill scholar, member of the National Society of the Daughters of the American Revolution.

Natyzak, Debra. Founder and president of the Frelinghuysen Township Historical Society.

Norato, Jennifer Dowling. Peer editor for this book; former chapter regent, Daughters of the American Revolution; New Jersey chapter president of the Alexander Hamilton Awareness Society.

Norwood, The Reverend John R., PhD. Pastor of Ujima Village Christian Church, Nanticoke Lenni-Lenape Tribal Nation of Southern New Jersey.

Peck, Donald Johnstone. Historian and author.

Pierson, George C. Historical Society of Scotch Plains and Fanwood.

Polhamus, Nancy. Gloucester County Library System, Mullica Hill.

Polhemus, Doreen. Millstone Township historian, Friends of Millstone Township Registered Historic Properties.

Price, Barbara. Library staff. Gloucester County Historical Society, Woodbury.

Putman, Tyler. Senior manager of gallery interpretation at the Museum of the American Revolution in Philadelphia.

Robinson, Pam, and David Harding. Hunterdon County Historical Society.

Roth, Steven. Author, New Jersey Postal History Society.

Rottweiler, Wendi. Local history librarian, Woodbridge Public Library.

Schriek, Robert, and Susan Allen. Library of the Chathams.

Schwertfeger, Rick. The *Frontier Partisans Southern Command*.

Sery, Jim and Nancy. Current owners of the old Death of the Fox Tavern.

Shankman, Andrew. Editor of the *Journal of the Early Republic*, professor of history at Rutgers University–Camden.

Sherblom, Donald E. 1759 Vought House group.

Simon, Susan, and Nikolina Uzicainin. Madison Historical Society.

Smith, Audrey. Cranbury Historical and Preservation Society.

Smith, Margaret. Program director, Readington Museums.

Solomon, Jessica. Executive director, Jewish Heritage Museum of Monmouth.

Stevens, Stephanie B. Historian for the County of Hunterdon and the Township of Readington.

Szypszak, Lara S. Library of Congress.

Tettamanti, Steven. Executive director, New Jersey Historical Society.

Thomson, W. Barry. Historian, author, trustee of the Historical Society of Somerset Hills.

Vohden, Richard. Owner of Pequest Valley Farms in Green Township, member of the Green Township Historical Society.

Welsch, Bill. President, American Revolution Round Table of Richmond, Virginia.

Worrell, Deena. Gloucester City Library.

INDEX

ABOUT THE AUTHOR

Photo by Linda Buset.

This is Michael C. Gabriele's fifth book on New Jersey history, all published by Arcadia Publishing/The History Press. His previous books are, in chronological order: *The Golden Age of Bicycle Racing in New Jersey* (2011); *The History of Diners in New Jersey* (2013); *New Jersey Folk Revival Music: History and Tradition* (2016); and *Stories from New Jersey Diners: Monuments to Community* (2019). A lifelong Garden State resident, he is a 1975 graduate of Montclair State University and has worked as a journalist, freelance writer and author for more than forty years. Gabriele is a member of the board of trustees for the New Jersey Folk Festival at Rutgers University and a member of the executive boards for the Allied Artists of America, New York; the Nutley Historical Society; and the Theater League of Clifton, and he serves on the advisory board of the Clifton Arts Center.

Visit us at
www.historypress.com